THE TEN ESSENTIAL QUALITIES OF
AN UNDERWATER DEMOLITION MAN

PRIDE   IN YOUR SELF, IN YOUR TEAM, IN THE. AMPHIBIOUS FORCE AND IN THE NAVY, AND MOST IMPORTANT, PRIDE IN DEVELOPING THE SAME PRIDE IN SUBORDI-NATES.

LOYALTY   UP AND DOWN, IN ACTION AND WORD.

SINCERITY   IN ALL YOU DO.

RESPONSIBILITY   YOU HAVE IT—ACT ACCORDINGLY, AND LIVE UP TO IT.

LEADERSHIP   YOU ARE THE LEADER IN TITLE,—BE SURE YOU ARE IN DEED.

EXAMPLE   YOU ALWAYS SET IT—BE SURE IT'S GOOD.

FORETHOUGHT   CULTIVATE THE HABIT—AND EXERCISE IT.

FAIRNESS   BE ABSOLUTELY FAIR AND SQUARE WITH SUBORD-INATES—THERE IS NO OTHER STANDARD.

SEAMANSHIP   ONLY A MAN WHO IS A COMPETENT SEAMAN CAN TRULY COMMAND RESPECT.

COMMON SENSE   USE IT—THERE IS NO SUBSTITUTE.

I EXPECT THESE QUALITIES OF EVERY UNDERWATER DEMOLITION MAN, AND I EXPECT EACH OFFICER TO PUNCTILIOUSLY REQUIRE THESE QUALITIES OF ALL SUBORDINATES.

THIS FORCE HAS NO EQUAL. I, THEREFORE, EXPECT, AND WILL ONLY ACCEPT, THE BEST OF ALL MY MEN.

F. R. KAINE
LCDR U.S.N.R.
CO. UDT — 21

WALKING
IN
MUD

WALKING
IN
MUD

A Navy SEAL's
10 Rules for Surviving
the New Normal

STEVE GIBLIN

WITH JON LAND

Post Hill
PRESS

A POST HILL PRESS BOOK

Walking in Mud:
A Navy SEAL's 10 Rules for Surviving the New Normal
© 2021 by Steve Giblin with Jon Land
All Rights Reserved

ISBN: 978-1-63758-064-6
ISBN (eBook): 978-1-63758-065-3

Cover design by Cody Corcoran
Interior design and composition by Greg Johnson, Textbook Perfect

Post Hill Press
New York • Nashville
posthillpress.com

Published in the United States of America
1 2 3 4 5 6 7 8 9 10

I dedicate this book to the first line health care workers, the survivors, and the victims of the pandemic, as well as all their families.

Also, to my family—especially my wife Barbara, my children Tom, Taylor, Tori, and Sydney, my father Paul and mother Judy, and my stepmother Joyce.

To my friends, Teammates and Naval Special Warfare writ large for my special career in the Teams and those who raised me and also rode the ride with me, but more importantly the ones who were my FNG's and ultimately did the real heavy lifting in Afghanistan, Iraq, and the greater Global War on Terrorism.

To Tommy Valentine, Danny Deitz, Michael Murphy, "Axe," and the many more heroes who've made the ultimate sacrifice in training and in combat. I think about you every day. If not for all of you I wouldn't be who I am. Thank you.

The journey of a thousand miles begins with one step.

—LAO TZU

Contents

FORETHOUGHT

COMMON SENSE

Preface

Well, here we are. The long shadow of COVID-19 is at last receding, bringing brighter days with it.

But how bright?

"Our best guess is something like 60 percent of the employment reduction is going to be temporary, and 40 percent is going to be permanent," Nicholas Bloom, an economics professor at Stanford University, told Marketplace.org last May. "Looking through history at previous recessions, often these temporary layoffs unfortunately turn out to be permanent."

And, according to AARP, "COVID-19 will change everything, from how we greet each other to what's on our bucket list. 'It's the single greatest disruption of our lifetime,' says Jeffrey Cole, director of the Center for the Digital Future at the University of Southern California. 'The kind of change that's occurred over a few months will change how we do things for years.'"

Pharmafield, in an article titled "New Normal, New Thinking: Life Post COVID-19," adds, "The COVID-19 pandemic has changed, and will continue to change, the world and the way we work, rest and play. So 'going back' to the way we were before COVID-19 is not an option. The challenge, and I think the opportunity, is now to start the process of thinking about a 'new normal.'"

Ian Davis from McKinsey & Company said this in that same article: "What will normal look like? While no one can say how long the crisis will last, what we find on the other side will not look like the normal of recent years."

The point is the light breaking through the clouds of COVID may not burn as bright for everyone. Indeed, the effects and realities imposed upon us by the New Normal are likely to have ramifications for everyone (some more than others). I faced plenty of metaphorical clouds in my twenty-six years as a Navy SEAL, and my goal in the pages that follow is to provide you with time-tested tools to deal with whatever shape the New Normal takes and what that means for you.

So why is this book so damn important to me, and why did I feel the need to intertwine my life story and experiences, as well as those of a few others, into a guide for surviving the post-pandemic world, this New Normal in which we find ourselves? My goal, my purpose, is to get a message out that's been gnawing at me for several years, even before the pandemic struck.

For many people, everyday life has been getting more and more polarized. Politics is dividing friendships, families, and workplaces. The news has become an either/or predicament: either you believe this or you believe that, with nothing in the middle. We have our left- and right-wing news agencies, and they feed us conflicting news that spins it into the narrative they want us to hear.

This naturally divides us into subgroups of Americans, and it has transformed our sense of collective identity into competing camps. It's become a way of life, permeating and influencing our conversations, the people and groups we associate with, the shows we watch, and, hell, even the places we eat out at. Yes, now there are restaurants that have made public their moral or ethical beliefs, and that has created factions of people who either will eat there because they agree with the mindset or those who will not come hell or high water; they'd rather starve.

Amazing! Even eating has become polarized!

More recently, we've all witnessed the competing viewpoints of maskers and the non-maskers, the vaxxers and the anti-vaxxers. All the contention and conflict that was present prior to the virus has only been inflamed by the social, economic, and practical changes imposed upon us in this New Normal fostered by COVID-19. To put it in US Navy SEAL terms, the virus has left us walking in mud on the bottom of a dark bay carrying a heavy load while breathing from a scuba tank. And as a former SEAL, I find myself wanting to help make sense of this unexpected burden we're all living with by sharing some of my own experiences and how they relate to what the whole country is facing.

Many of you have no doubt heard of the infamous BUD/S bell that hangs outside the training cadre's office. You ring it once to get the attention of the cadre inside. Ringing it three times triggers a "Drop on Request," meaning you quit. Once rung, you can never "un-ring" the bell. I think all of us at some point in the months since COVID hit have wanted to ring our own metaphorical bell three times. To throw up our hands in the face of overwhelming adversity and changes forced upon us that we neither embraced nor signed up for. As much as anything, the mission statement for this book is to provide an alternative to ringing the bell when life piles on, if not because of COVID, then because of something else. And, unlike the case in BUD/S, you can indeed "un-ring" your metaphorical bell and this book will help you there, too, in steering a course toward recovery, reconstruction, and, even, redemption.

How do we get out of the figurative mud in which we find our feet mired, slogging along with every step a challenge? That's the question. For the answers, turn the page, and let's begin our journey to the other side.

Introduction

To augment present naval capabilities in restricted waters
and rivers with particular reference to the conduct and
support of paramilitary operations, it is desirable to establish
Special Operations teams as a separate component within
Underwater Demolition Units One and Two.
An appropriate cover name for such units is 'SEAL'
being a contraction of SEA, AIR, LAND.

—VICE ADM. WALLACE M. BEAKLEY,
Deputy Chief of Naval Operations, June 5, 1961

I wasn't born until two years after Vice Admiral Wallace Beakley uttered those words that would come to define my adult life. I loved every minute of being a Navy SEAL and served in Special Operations for twenty-six years, fourteen of those (1987–2001) with Naval Special Warfare Development Group.

As a SEAL I traveled all over the world to train with our allies and fight America's enemies, never imagining that the greatest enemy, and greatest challenge, our country ever faced would end up being something I couldn't even see. A microbe, a virus.

COVID-19.

As individuals, we never could have anticipated or prepared for this. One day the world was normal and the next everything changed, jolted to a halt by the pandemic. Part of my training as a

SEAL involved preparing for biological warfare, but no enemy I'd been trained to fight unleashed this scourge upon us. There are the theories as to how it came to be, but at this point it doesn't really matter. This virus knows no nationality, culture, or political persuasion. COVID-19 has upended our lives, confronted us with our own mortality, and torn apart the very fabric of who we are.

Not being one to give in or give up, I found myself wanting to respond, not with bullets but a keyboard. My job, my purpose, as a Navy SEAL was to keep you safe from the things that go bump in the night, from the monsters out there that are very real. COVID is a monster too. And if I can't keep you safe from it, maybe I can at least help you endure the New Normal the pandemic has left in its wake. To foster a mindset of perseverance, of courage, of never giving up in the face of adversity—the bedrock principles of the Navy SEALs.

First, a bit of perspective.

In 1983, the Naval Special Warfare community was going through its biggest reorganization since the early 1960s and Vietnam, which established SEAL Teams 1 and 2. Underwater Demolition Teams (UDTs) were being transitioned over to SEAL Teams and Swimmer Delivery Vehicle Teams (SDVTs, later to change to SEAL Delivery Vehicle Teams). On the West Coast, SEAL Teams 3 and 5 and SDVT-1 were born and Underwater Demolition Teams 11 and 12 were disestablished. On the East Coast, meanwhile, SEAL Team 4 and SDVT-2 were born and UDTs 21 and 22 were disestablished.

"In January 1962, a new chapter in the history of special operations opened with the establishment of the U.S. Navy's SEAL Teams ONE and TWO," Jon Dwight Zimmerman wrote for the Defense Media Network in December of 2011. "The 21-year stretch from 1962 to 1983 was a profound one for the new force, one that would see it created from the Navy's Underwater Demolition

Teams (UDTs) and grow to a point where, in 1983, the parent organization would be folded into that of its offspring."

The East Coast Teams also saw a new compound get constructed to house the two newly established Teams and SEAL Team 2. All three Teams were quite a distance apart from one another on the amphibious base. SEAL Team 2 was near the housing units, SEAL Team 4 was near the dining facility and base fire station, and SDVT-2 was where the magazines and Special Boat Unit 20 were located.

The West Coast Teams would stay where they were, co-located on the Silver Strand side of the amphibious base with the exception of SDVT-1. They would remain on the main side of base, next door to Special Boat Unit 12 (now Special Boat Team 12). Both SDV Teams needed proximity and access to the respective bays that their bases sat on in order to launch and recover the SDVs and support craft. A SEAL Team, on the other hand, could be almost anywhere on base since they weren't so dependent on the required equipment that the SDV Teams were.

My BUD/S class, 124, was one of the first to be assigned to the newly established Teams. The classes before us that year received orders to UDTs or SEAL Team 1 or 2, although the UDTs transitioned into the new framework later that year for them. Be that as it may, we were all still FNGs (fucking new guys) in the world of Frogmen and SEALs, which are one and the same.

As FNGs, we were the designated personnel who would pack up the equipment of the UDT and either move it to the new Team area, get rid of it at the base dump, or place it with the Defense Reutilization and Marketing Service (DRMO) where the stuff would get turned around and used again. This included even the old Vietnam-era office furniture, the desks and file cabinets and all that, which was getting replaced with brand-new furniture.

I was assigned to clean out the front office where the Team's commanding officer, executive officer, Command Master Chief, and operations officer were located. They had already packed their personal effects, but there was still plenty to clean up. As for all the old classified papers and files, they were to be put into burn bags and sent to the base incinerator where they could be destroyed properly and in accordance with Department of Defense (DoD) policy at the time.

I was going through everything I was told to and sorting it all out to be either destroyed, put into the trash, or kept for reuse. That's when I found the one-page document that forms the basis of this book, the Ten Essential Qualities of an Underwater Demolition Man, tucked way back in a drawer and left behind by the Team commanding officer who had vacated the office.

Here are those Ten Qualities, reproduced from the original document that I've kept close to me ever since the day I found it.

The Ten Essential Qualities of an Underwater Demolition Man

PRIDE: In yourself, in your team, in the amphibious force and in the Navy, and most important, pride in developing the same pride in subordinates.

LOYALTY: Up and down, in action and word.

SINCERITY: In all you do.

RESPONSIBILITY: You have it—act accordingly, and live up to it.

LEADERSHIP: You are the leader in title—be sure you are in deed.

EXAMPLE: You always set it—be sure it's good.

FORETHOUGHT: Cultivate the habit—and exercise it.

FAIRNESS: Be absolutely fair and square with subordinates—there is no other standard.

SEAMANSHIP: Only a man who is a competent seaman can truly command respect.

COMMON SENSE: Use it—there is no substitute.

LCDR F.R. Kaine, U.S.N.R.,
Commanding Officer,
Underwater Demolition Team-21

These were the simple expectations that then Commanding Officer Francis Kaine of Underwater Demolition Team 21 (UDT-21) expected from his operators. This document found its way into my hot little hands, and I've never come across another man with a copy of the same.

There was nothing else I found that week that would last the length of my career like that single piece of paper would. It has remained close to my heart and never far from my thoughts through all the years since—the hard copy accompanying me on all the moves I've made from that day I first came upon it until today—and today is what *Walking in Mud* is all about. We are dealing with the residue of the greatest attack the United States has ever faced, undertaken by an invisible, insidious enemy.

As of this writing, over 610,000 Americans have perished to COVID-19. That's more than the sum total of American lives claimed from both World War I and World War II combined—all in little more than a year to an enemy we can't even see, much less fight. I served as an operator in Special Operations alongside some of the best-trained warriors in the world, but even my brothers and I couldn't stand up to this virus. It is nothing like the traditional sorts of enemies we faced as we carried out our missions.

But in the midst of the pandemic, something occurred to me. Having lived with the Ten Essential Qualities of an Underwater Demolition Man for the better part of my life, I was struck by how those rules, those qualities, apply to the world in which we find ourselves now. A world where nothing is the same as it was going back to the early months of 2020 and might well never be the same for the rest of our lifetimes and beyond.

I can't change that; I wish I could, but I can't. What I can do, though, is show you how those Ten Qualities that have been so vital to me in how I try to live my life can be equally vital for you.

Since this book had to be completed months before its publication date, the statistics and data I quote may not be totally up to date. What is up to date, though, is the thinking I hope the Ten Qualities will help instill in you. Indeed, because we are living in a new world, many of us need a new way of thinking.

"The world as we have created it is a process of our thinking," Albert Einstein once said. "It cannot be changed without changing our thinking."

But *Walking in Mud* isn't about changing the world; it's about changing yourself to better enable you to confront the New Normal. That term will mean something different to everyone who reads this book, but in facing it, in persevering in the New Normal, it's my deepest hope that the Ten Essential Qualities of an Underwater Demolition Man will apply to all. Maybe a little, maybe a lot.

"In much of what SEALs do, it's learn as you go," Rear Admiral George Worthington said when he was a "mere" lieutenant commander. "Adaptability is the name of the game."

I've taken my own experiences as a SEAL, as well as from my life before and after, to provide context for each of the Ten Essential Qualities, representing how each can be applied to what you're experiencing today. Because right now we're all walking in mud, jammed in ruts and slogging through muck that was neither our making nor anything we can control. What we *can* control is how we respond to the pandemic and the residue it's left on our lives. The Ten Qualities, and their respective applications, are not presented in the same order as they appear in the original document because I believe Commander Kaine viewed them as having equal importance and relevance. So, the order doesn't matter; what matters is that you follow them the same way I've been doing for nearly forty years.

I'd pick you up and carry you out of the proverbial mud if I could, the same way I did on more than one occasion for a SEAL

Teammate. I can't do that, but I can offer myself up as a guide to help you find firmer ground that gets you to the other side. That's what those Ten Qualities are all about, and that's what this book is all about.

First, though, I think it would only be fair to share a little about myself.

My Time in the Teams

True happiness is to enjoy the present, without anxious dependence upon the future, not to amuse ourselves with either hopes or fears but to rest satisfied with what we have, which is sufficient, for he that is so wants nothing. The greatest blessings of mankind are within us and within our reach. A wise man is content with his lot, whatever it may be, without wishing for what he has not.

—SENECA

I'd like you to get to know me, or at least understand where I'm coming from. I've come to accept my lot and am proud of my service, both in uniform and as a civilian. I haven't always acted honorably or committed to virtues that help to define a man, but I've recognized that flaw and work every day to become a better man, a better human.

Life is dynamic, not static. The events of today are not necessarily a precursor for tomorrow. That's a fact as well as a metaphor because if I've learned nothing else in life, it's that change is the only constant. We've all experienced that these past few years—for the worse, unfortunately. But better days are already upon us and, more than anything, the mission statement of this book is for you to focus on what's coming as opposed to what's already been. We can't change that. But the days to come—that's something else again.

If I were to write a letter to my seventeen-year-old self, it would say something to the effect of, "Steve, you're going to be wild and impulsive and, at times, take an unconventional path in life. You will take risks, both personal and professional. Settle down and think before you act; don't be so thoughtless. Don't fall in love with every girl you meet; the right one will find you. Seek a mentor, always. Mentor others, often. Be a decent human being. Be humble and take ownership of everything you do, professionally and personally."

I'm not the kind of SEAL who went out and killed a bunch of bad guys on hair-raising missions. Yes, I trained, deployed, and was gone from home for more than two-thirds of my career, but I feel I was born one decade too early, putting me out of sync with the combat every Frogman wants and signs up for. Perhaps this is what was intended, my lot in life. Someone had to "grind it through the '90s," as a buddy of mine would say.

I've accepted that it wasn't meant for me to be that operator who everyone expects a SEAL to be—to have been everywhere and killed everything in sight. I saw combat in Panama; I was part of operations in Bosnia, Somalia, and Iraq. But they weren't the kind of operations that everyone envisions or sees on TV and the movies. I've got a rack of ribbons and medals, but no Bronze Star Medal or "V" for Valor on any of the commendation medals that ride below the Trident that I wore.

I've got buddies who saw heavy combat. I've lost friends and Teammates in combat and in training. I've got some friends who almost died and one who actually flatlined on the table and came back from it, and still deployed afterward. In the Teams and Special Operations, it's all about timing and luck.

2

I've got a friend, Teammate, and contemporary whose timing always seemed perfect and was blessed with stellar luck, as far as operators from my generation go. Pat has seen way more combat than any single operator should get to see. Luck and timing have most to do with it, but in that same breath he positioned himself so he could do that. He made sacrifices and dedicated himself to the trade of being an operator almost to a fault. He was in Grenada, Lebanon, Panama, Bosnia, Afghanistan, and Iraq, to name just a few areas of operations.

Pat works with the three-letter guys doing what you think a guy like that should do. I've still got friends in that organization, as well as at the Special Mission Unit and other SEAL Teams. Just about all of them are older, senior guys now, salty. A couple were either on, or heavily involved with, key raids and hostage rescue operations over the past two decades. All were junior to me, some worked for me, and some I helped train. Like I said, I was born a generation late and my timing was off. I still had luck, though, but in other ways.

I served twenty-eight years in the US Navy, twenty-six of which were spent in Naval Special Warfare and the SEAL Teams under the United States Special Operations Command (USSOCOM). I enlisted in the Navy in 1981 at seventeen years old, two months out of high school. For those two months between high school and the Navy, I had worked in a wrecking yard on the outskirts of Albuquerque in the body shop rebuilding cars that would be sold to unwitting customers thinking the vehicle was only used and not a salvage. It would involve removing the damaged parts like a fender or hood and replacing them with parts from salvaged wrecks, sometimes going to the extreme and cutting off the front end entirely and replacing it with the same model from another wreck with its tail end crushed.

My days in the shop were spent welding, grinding, sanding, repainting, and polishing. It was tedious and mind-numbing, more than enough to convince me that I wanted more from my life at that time; stitching cars back together didn't cut it as my purpose. I needed some adventure, and working with a couple of burnouts rebuilding wrecks six days a week and being their "shop boy" wasn't my idea of adventure at the time. I didn't want to be like them in ten or fifteen years.

Becoming a SEAL for me started in boot camp. We had a physical training instructor wearing this blue-and-gold shirt that read UDT/SEAL INSTRUCTOR. He reminded me of my dad in a way. Very fit and confident. In the first week, after I smoked the initial Navy physical fitness tests, he pulled me aside.

"What are you gonna do in my Navy, son?" he asked me.

"I'm supposed to go into aviation, serve on an aircraft carrier."

"Are you interested in becoming a Frogman?"

That was the first time I'd ever heard the word, but the instructor proceeded to tell me all about the SEALs and showed me a short movie, *The Men with Green Faces*. I was hooked from the get-go. Every other Wednesday during basic training, before the day started, I'd show up to do the screening test for BUD/S (SEAL basic training) just to get more physical training in and to show this guy I wanted in. My company commander blew his lid when he found out what I was doing.

"They're all fucking crazy," he told me.

"Okay," I said. "I want to lose my mind."

Boot camp was at a naval training facility in San Diego, California, which has since been replaced by a residential development known as Liberty Station. It hosts a Trader Joe's and scores of niche restaurants and shops these days. Up until that point in 1981, I had never heard of the SEAL Teams, Frogmen, or any of that. I joined the Navy to serve, see the world, and hopefully grow the hell up.

I served my first year and a half in the Navy with the Fleet aboard the carrier USS *Ranger* home ported in San Diego as an undesignated airman, an E-2 and then E-3. I made one WESTPAC

(Western Pacific) tour in 1982 and worked on the flight deck, catapults and arresting gear division, launching fighter jets and surveillance aircraft.

We deployed to the Western Pacific and Indian Ocean areas of responsibility (AOR) and worked sixteen hours Monday through Saturday and eight on Sunday while at sea. We hit the ports of the Philippines (twice), Singapore, and Australia. I turned eighteen that year and had way, way, way too much fun. The work was harder than back in the salvage yard, but this seemed to suit me better, this life in the Navy.

In 1983, after returning to San Diego from WESTPAC, I was graciously allowed to depart the ship early, against the conventional rules of the Navy, terminating that tour early after receiving a new set of orders to attend Basic Underwater Demolition/SEAL Training (BUD/S), where we learned the very basics of being a Frogman and SEAL operator. I was in a class that started with 130 or so trainees and graduated with twenty-seven, twenty-four of whom were originals including myself. (The other three were "roll backs," picking up their training after being injured in a previous class.)

My first assignment out of BUD/S and in the Teams was at SEAL Delivery Vehicle Team 2 (SDVT-2) from 1983 to 1987 at Naval Amphibious Base Little Creek in Virginia Beach. The Team had just transitioned from Underwater Demolition Team 22 (UDT-22) that same year as part of a reorganization meant to bring the Teams out of the '70s and into a new era.

I was still a teenager, all of nineteen, when I checked into my first Team. The very first morning at quarters I met a salty Frogman Master Chief named Ed Schmidt. He was from a completely different era. When he was a nineteen-year-old FNG, it was World War II and he was swimming across the beaches of Normandy, Sicily, and Africa. He was originally NCDU, Naval Combat Demolition Unit, and was trained at Fort Pierce, Florida. He had a swagger to him, an extreme air of confidence. You could see the experience in his eyes and the lines on his face as he chewed on his toothpick. He had broken service, missed Korea, but came back in right at the beginning of the Vietnam conflict. He was an early member of SEAL Team 2 and made several deployments to the Mekong Delta.

I wanted to be just like this guy.

In those four years at SDVT-2, I served and deployed with three platoons. Back then you did quick turnarounds—a six-month or less pre-deployment training and then six-month deployments as opposed to the two-year cycle for each platoon today. That said, the current model is now very predictable and conducive to today's military lifestyle. An operator will spend six years at his first Team, still getting three pumps overseas, but he will be better trained and probably more stable with regard to where he's going and confident about the skills he's acquiring for the job.

Three months after checking in and just before my first platoon, I went to SDV school (located back then in Coronado, California) for three months, which you'll read about later in the book. In my first platoon, myself and four other FNGs deployed without our Tridents. We hadn't gone through our advanced operator training within the Team yet in order to earn the "Budweiser" or SEAL pin, our Navy Enlisted Classification (NEC), and get the extra pay. Funny how we weren't "qualified" yet, but we were still good enough to deploy overseas and perform Frogman duties.

In 1989, Petty Officer Second Class Isaac Rodriguez was fresh out of BUD/S and deployed to Panama for Operation Just Cause, where he was KIA (killed in action) at Paitilla Airfield. He hadn't earned his Trident yet either, but they threw him into a platoon and into combat. That was how things went back in the '80s. It was okay to just be good enough.

Within our tight-knit platoons, we were taught a lot of advanced skills by our leadership and more experienced operators, some of whom were veterans of Vietnam. That first platoon wasn't a combat deployment, so we had plenty of time to train and learn. We went to Denmark for six weeks to work with the Danish Frogmen and to participate in a major exercise, then on to the UK for a month or so to work with the Special Boat Service (SBS) before returning home. We were only gone for about three months, but it was a great experience and left me wanting more.

When we got back to the States, we were assigned to the training platoon (along with other FNGs and SEALs newly attached to our Team) where we learned the advanced operator skills required to be "qualified" for an SDV platoon and for us new guys to earn our Tridents. Our mission was primarily focused on undersea and near-shore operations. We trained with explosives and small arms and spent hours upon hours perfecting our tradecraft as Frogmen. Our dives with the SDV would be anywhere from four hours in the cold springtime water to ten-plus hours in the summer waters of Chesapeake Bay.

If we were lucky, our next platoon would deploy to the Naval Special Warfare (NSW) unit in Puerto Rico for the winter pre-deployment training and dive in the warm waters of the Caribbean. I did that twice while at the SDV Team and plenty more times at my next Team.

I deployed to the Caribbean and the Mediterranean twice on various Navy platforms, everything from an amphibious ship to a diving salvage ship to an SSN, a submarine outfitted with our mission-specific equipment. During my second and third deployments, there were contingencies that we were spun up for but we never acted on. This is why the Navy is deployed around the world, in every sea and ocean. The United States supports and protects our national interests as well as our allies, but the American public doesn't always see these small contingencies or low-intensity operations. When the United States attacked Libya during Operation El Dorado Canyon, for example, there were SEALs and Marines on standby, waiting just off the coast, to help in any way possible whether it be personnel rescue or otherwise...just in case.

Just before I departed for my third deployment in January 1987, I screened (interviewed) for DevGru and was accepted to the next Green Team set for July of that same year. DevGru, by the way, is short for Naval Special Warfare Development Group (NSWDG, or DEVelopment GRoUp). It's the NSW component of the Joint Special Operations Command (JSOC). The unit is often referred to within JSOC as Task Force Blue, and it's where I spent the next fourteen years (1987–2001) at the Special Mission Unit as an operator, trainer, and enlisted leader.

I had left the SDV team as a frocked E-5—not exactly a "rate grabber" for a guy with six years in the Navy. But I made up for that once assigned to DevGru. I transferred from that command on August 3, 2001, just six or so weeks before 9/11, the biggest tragedy of our generation in the US and one month past my twenty-year anniversary in the Navy.

In my time at DevGru, I was fortunate enough to be mentored by some of the best in our community and work my way up the chain of command until I became an Assault Team Chief, the senior enlisted for my particular assault team. At that time, I was one of three at DevGru and one of six in the United States, 1st Special Forces Operational Detachment—Delta (SFOD-D, a.k.a. Delta Force) having the other three. My Team Leader and I led a sixty-five-man assault force for national-level missions. These days, both commands have grown one more assault squadron and have been heavily involved in steady combat operations over the last two decades, since October of 2001, more than anyone ever imagined.

In the SEAL Teams, DevGru is the place most guys want to eventually be. Not all get that opportunity and of those that do, some don't make it past the initial assessment and selection for Green Team. It's a selection course for the most extreme operations anyone can ever imagine. Six months of some of the most intense combat training an operator could receive. Some guys are up for it and some are not. I was "all in" and fortunate to have been allowed to serve for the time that I did.

Not every SEAL wants to be there, for their own reasons, and I've got all the respect in the world for those guys. Many of them are friends of mine, and they're good Frogmen in their own right and have done great things and have seen a lot of combat. But come 2001, I felt like someone had thrown me off the bullet train and I was skidding to an abrupt halt. Assholes over elbows and shit flying off everywhere. My world seemed to be upended from what I had known for the last two decades, something that would happen again eight years later.

After I was unceremoniously let go from DevGru in August of 2001 (more on this later), I was assigned to Naval Special Warfare Group 2/Training Detachment 2 (NSWG-2/TRADET-2). I wouldn't necessarily say I was floundering at that point, but I felt I still had a lot to give, a lot to contribute. Toward that end, what I really needed to do was to find another mentor. Someone who could help get my head straight and give me some solid advice about finding the best path available to me. This is all in hindsight, though, and I ultimately never sought nor found one. Instead, I trudged on in my own self-pity and mud, walking on the bottom of the bay without a dive buddy, so to speak. And I never found that path.

Initially, at the TRADET, I was the Assault Cell Senior Enlisted and Instructor. Our job was to train the SEAL platoons in urban combat, close-quarter combat, shipboard assaults, and tactical vehicle operations. I was there to teach everything I had learned and experienced at my previous command. I was a Senior Chief managing a ten-man training cell, a far cry from leading the sixty-five-man assault team I'd just left, but I was still in the Teams and still giving a shit.

The summer I left DevGru I was a thirty-seven-year-old Senior Chief with twenty years in and had decisions to make in my life. Friends of mine were retiring or just leaving the Navy to go work for the three-letter guys to fight the war, and they were doing their best to convince me to do the same. I was torn, but I stayed because I felt I still had more to do, more to offer, and I owed my Teammates, the NSW community, and the service that supported me. My marriage was in trouble as well, and I felt I needed to pay attention to that or risk losing it.

I shredded my retirement request that sat in my truck, after staring at the paperwork for weeks, and stayed on for another eight years. I was promoted to Master Chief the following spring and was put in charge, as the senior enlisted, of the entire training detachment for a short time.

My officer in charge (OIC) and I managed sixty-five SEAL instructors and support personnel. The detachment trained two-hundred-plus SEALs annually for combat deployments and other overseas deployments and operations. We were a bunch of seasoned operators who only wanted to deploy into the new combat zone of Afghanistan, the "GWOT" (Global War on Terrorism, pronounced "gee-what"), but were now supposed to train the guys who were going to do that. Not a good time to be in the "trainer" position when your Teammates and country are at war, and keeping our guys focused was, at the very least, a challenge. Had we known that the war would drag on for as long as it has, maybe we wouldn't have been so impatient.

That point in my career was the closest I had come to shore duty, a tour where you don't deploy or aren't on a short leash to go forward, to go overseas. My Navy and Special Operations deployment experience had taken me to the Western Pacific, Caribbean, North Atlantic, Mediterranean, Europe, and Central America. Some were routine deployments and others for contingency operations in numerous countries for a myriad of reasons.

Things changed for me again within the next twelve months. I was selected and assigned to be a Command Master Chief (CMC) for SEAL Delivery Vehicle Team 2, the East Coast undersea Special Operations combat arm of Naval Special Warfare. The same command I started my Frogman career at, the sometimes forgotten and always underrated Team who continue to get the job done quietly and without fanfare. I was the CMC for the very men for whom those Ten Essential Qualities of an Underwater Demolition Man had been written—real Frogmen.

My tour at the Team as CMC was good. As the undersea team we did the Frogman mission first, ground operations second. A tough spot to be in, though, when we were at war in the barren Middle East; not much water to be found in Afghanistan, either, and very little in Iraq.

Getting the operators, the SEALs, into the fight in the Middle East was a tough sell to the upper echelons. They were assigned to a mission that didn't prioritize ground combat operations, even though half of the operators came from a SEAL Team. We had more snipers, more Joint Terminal Attack Controllers and other tactical communicators at the time due to our command's mission priority for the reconnaissance elements that operated from the SDVs. They specialized in special reconnaissance in harbors and over the beach into the near shore area as four-man teams. They finally deployed in direct combat operations in Afghanistan and Iraq and did great things alongside their fellow SEALs, conducting sniper missions, special reconnaissance, and target assaults.

We also had tragedies. Petty Officer Danny Dietz was one who died alongside Petty Officer Matt Axelson and Lieutenant Michael Murphy during Operation Red Wings. Nobody signs up to die; we do it for the honor and privilege to defend our nation in a specialized organization. This happened in the final months of my CMC tour before transferring to the West Coast for another CMC tour.

I only deployed twice more after I pinned on Master Chief, once to Africa as a task force senior enlisted while at the SDV Team and then to Iraq when I was finally at my first and only shore duty during the surge of 2007–2008.

After I returned from Iraq, my chain of command wanted more from me. My Force Master Chief called and emailed me while I was still in Iraq and was pressuring me to take orders to Special Operations Command Korea (SOCKOR) as the Senior Enlisted Advisor (SEA) to the commander there. That would mean two to three more years away from my second wife, and since she had her own career and my stepdaughter was well established in the local high school, I faced a dilemma. My own daughters from my first marriage lived in Virginia. I already rarely saw them and wouldn't see them at all for a long stretch during that tour if I took it. That would have also meant not being engaged in the fight again. I did my best to convince the higher-ups I would deploy again for another six-month pump to the Middle East as an operations guy, a SEAL, or water boy—I didn't care—but to no avail.

I even volunteered to take a fellow Master Chief's place as the SEA in the Horn of Africa for a one-year tour. We were getting heavily engaged in the region, and I wanted to be a part of that as a follow-up to my 2003 deployment there. My buddy had a son with medical issues, so me coming in to replace him seemed like a win-win, but our Force Master Chief and admiral didn't see it that way and refused.

Here I was, at a crossroads again. Capitulate and go to Korea, or retire and leave the life I'd loved through twenty-eight years of service. I didn't have intentions of retiring that soon, but the road to hell is paved with good intentions, as they say.

I felt I was being sidelined for some things I had said and done in the years past. My admiral called me, the same man I worked for in Iraq and had known since the 1980s. He tried to convince me to go to Korea; he said he needed me there, that NSW needed me there. I asked him, if he were in my position, whether he would do that or anything and everything possible to get into the fight. His reply was typical:

"It's not about me, Steve."

I told him I was done. He let me know that if I changed my mind, he would personally pull my retirement papers and I had some time to decide. This was November of 2008.

I decided that I needed to retire. Once that idea settled into my brain, I realized I was tired. The adrenaline, the rush, was gone and all that was left was exhaustion. I retired in July of 2009 from Naval Special Warfare Center in Coronado, twenty-eight years to the month after I entered the Navy at seventeen years old. It was a bittersweet departure, but one that left me reflecting on all I had learned.

Like the Ten Essential Qualities, these lessons have stuck with me. I wanted to share them with you so you might benefit from applying them to the New Normal.

So, in continuing this letter to myself, I wanted to focus on those lessons that have gained fresh efficacy in the world in which we find ourselves today:

- **Know your own competence.** Don't be arrogant. No one is perfect, and you need to operate within the boundaries of your own ability.

- **Let people be their true selves.** As a leader, you have a responsibility to create an environment where people don't feel like they have to pretend in order to fit in. It's okay if you don't know something. If you are trying to be the superhuman "I know everything" leader, you will fail.

- **Persuade through questions.** The best way to help someone see a different perspective is not to pound the table and berate them but rather ask thoughtful questions to help them understand your view.

- **Be mindful of how you present yourself.** Leadership is found in the tedious. No matter what stage in life you're in, you will be a leader. As a leader, people notice what you say and do all the time. Casual comments and actions will get noticed.

- **Get intimate with the lowest level.** As a leader, you need to know what it's like being on the line and getting your hands dirty. Know the job of everyone in your lineup not through "knowing" but by doing.

- **Control what you can.** The environment, the weather, and other people are things you cannot control. Those elements always get 51 percent of the vote. So, when things seem overwhelming, get hyper-focused on the small things within your circle of control. Become self-aware and concentrate on breathing and staying calm. You have no control over how the day unfolds for anyone else but yourself. Just be ready to react in a calm, cool manner.

- **Learn to visualize and self-talk.** Try to deconstruct decisions before the outcomes have occurred. Visualize the conversation or situation and all the possible outcomes to each scenario. This way, even when the unlikely happens, you're already prepared, and you don't overreact because you've thought about it in advance.

- **Let people vent.** Especially the ones you love. And when they do, truly listen. Some leaders usually think they have the solution to an individual's problem before they even talk. It's better to just be quiet and let them talk. Oftentimes, they don't need your advice. They just need you to listen.

- **Be open-minded to perspectives you disagree with.** Leadership is not being afraid to credit those with whom we often disagree.

- **Keep your word even if it doesn't benefit you.** Promises are sacred. Always stay true to your word, even if it turns out breaking it might benefit you more. If it isn't life threatening and won't bankrupt you, what's the harm? This is how you can become a trustworthy leader and better human. And when others look to you for help, they're helping you as much as themselves.

Throughout 2020, and now well into 2021, COVID-19 has dominated our lives, wrecked a lot of livelihoods, and left us questioning what our New Normal will look like. I could add *once the dust has settled*, except I don't know when that's going to happen or how much dust there's going to be clouding our vision and clogging up the works. I do know that we need to look ahead instead of back. The lessons above will help sharpen our vision in that respect, but the Ten Essential Qualities of an Underwater Demolition Man will provide the goals and targets to aim for. Because it's time to find a fresh outlook and forge a new beginning to get ourselves out of the muck in which we find ourselves lodged.

"New beginnings," Lao Tzu once wrote, "are often disguised as painful endings."

So, let's turn the page and begin to explore those new beginnings.

RESPONSIBILITY

Steve with his parents circa 1966

CHAPTER 1

Post-Traumatic Stress Disorder: An Epidemic in Its Own Right

Men, Special Forces is a mistress. Your wives will envy her because she will have your hearts. Your wives will be jealous of her because of the power to pull you away. This mistress will show you things never before seen and experience things never before felt. She will love you, but only a little, seducing you to want more, give more; die for her. She will take you away from the ones you love, and you will hate her for it, but leave her you never will, but if you must, you will miss her, for she has a part of you that will never be returned intact. And in the end, she will leave you for a younger man.

—JAMES R. WARD, OSS

That quote comes from a buddy of mine I served with on the Special Mission Unit under JSOC who's now an operator with the three-letter guys. I don't know if I've ever seen a more appropriate or accurate quote when it comes to serving in Special Operations. It highlights the constant push-pull between the call of duty to country and family. Both of those are awesome responsibilities, and successfully negotiating them requires a resilience seldom seen outside the world I spent twenty-six years in.

Until now.

Since COVID-19 first reared its ugly head, we have witnessed everyone becoming a warrior, not so much to survive as endure. The responsibility we bear to ourselves and our family is now cast in a new light. Think of the visions of lines at food banks and unemployment offices, undertaken by those swallowing their pride to fulfil their responsibilities and maintain the resilience that's vital to find the other side of the bog we've all been slogging through.

So, the mission statement of this initial chapter of the book will explore how to be responsible for ourselves so we can in turn be responsible for those who love us and depend on us. To a great degree, this means exercising the kind of resilience we'll all need to adjust to the New Normal that's been thrust upon us.

Resilience

The last year has bent all of us to varying degrees, but we can't let it break us. "Bamboo is flexible, bending with the wind but never breaking," the noted Chinese businesswoman Ping Fu has written, "capable of adapting to any circumstance. It suggests resilience, meaning that we have the ability to bounce back even from the most difficult times.... Your ability to thrive depends, in the end, on your attitude to your life circumstances. Take everything in stride with grace, putting forth energy when it is needed, yet always staying calm inwardly."

Easier said than done, I know.

The problem we face today, nearly two years into an assault on our sensibilities, health, and livelihoods, has left much of the nation reeling from what is essentially post-traumatic stress disorder (PTSD) too. It's something veterans like me know all too well from our own experience or that of the brothers and sisters we served with and leaves us uniquely suited to explain.

PTSD symptoms are generally grouped into four types: intrusive memories, avoidance, negative changes in thinking and mood, and changes in physical and emotional reactions. Symptoms can vary over time or vary from person to person.

According to USSOCOM records, there were 117 suicides among Special Operations forces (SOF) from 2007 to 2015, peaking at 23 in 2012—a rate of 39.3 per 100,000, compared with 22.9 per 100,000 for the US armed forces as a whole. The rate gradually declined after that, falling to eight cases in 2017. That year, one of the largest efforts to understand military suicide ever was undertaken, a study examining suicide attempts by personnel during the early years of the wars in Afghanistan and Iraq. It found that SOF might be more resilient than the general purpose forces because of "rigorous selection, intense training, strong unit cohesion or psychological and biological characteristics." The next year, SOF suicides spiked nearly threefold above 2017's total.

In other words, special operators like me aren't immune to the effects of PTSD. Nobody is.

"Since the coronavirus arrived," William Wan wrote in the *Washington Post* in November of 2020, "depression and anxiety in America have become rampant. Federal surveys show that 40 percent of Americans are now grappling with at least one mental health or drug-related problem. But young adults have been hit harder than any other age group, with 75 percent struggling. Even more alarming, when the Centers for Disease Control and Prevention recently asked young adults if they had thought about killing themselves in the past 30 days, 1 in 4 said they had. America's system for monitoring suicides is so broken and slow that experts won't know until roughly two years after the pandemic whether suicides have risen nationally. But what coroners and medical examiners are already seeing is troubling."

Further, the Centers for Disease Control and Prevention (CDC) reported in December of 2020 that "over 81,000 drug overdose deaths occurred in the United States in the 12 months ending in May 2020, the highest number of overdose deaths ever recorded in a 12-month period, according to recent provisional data...While overdose deaths were already increasing in the months preceding the 2019 novel coronavirus disease (COVID-19) pandemic, the latest numbers suggest an acceleration of overdose deaths during the pandemic.... Synthetic opioids (primarily illicitly manufactured fentanyl) appear to be the primary driver of the increases in overdose deaths, increasing 38.4 percent from the 12-month period leading up to June 2019 compared with the 12-month period leading up to May 2020."

Even toughened members of the SOF community can succumb to a sense of despair. A guy at my Team committed suicide on New Year's Eve, even though he was newly remarried and seemingly happy. His wife and daughter walked to the nearby store to pick up some dessert before the three of them snuggled in for the night to watch a movie and ring in the New Year. While they were gone, he walked out into the backyard with his .45, sat in a chair, and shot himself. Nobody knows why. Everyone struggled to understand and come to terms with this enormous loss. Nobody saw it coming and that's often, if not usually, the case.

There's something that lurks inside all of us. Call it a breaking point, and many who never thought they'd ever have to worry about such a thing have been experiencing it firsthand. In war people witness horrible things on the battlefield. Sometimes they're wounded, often seriously, and need medication just to make it through the day to deal with their physical pain. What we've all experienced these past nearly two years is more of an emotional pain, one no easier to treat, an anxiety that springs from the uncertainty of what's coming next. How will I survive financially? How can I afford the mortgage? What on earth will I do for a second act now that so much of what I knew has been stripped away from me? Uncertainty envelops our lives in a thick fog. The road ahead becomes blocked to our view. We can barely see the hand in front of our face. Every step becomes a struggle because we don't know what lies before us.

Before cell phones and built-in car navigation systems, many knew the empty feeling that comes with realizing that you're lost. You know where you're going but have lost the means to get there. The pandemic has spread that feeling to all facets of our life. College is still in your kids' future, but how are you going to pay for it? Retirement looms, but you've used up the funds put aside for that purpose to deal with the economic devastation wrought by the COVID crisis.

So, what do you do when walking in this particular mud? Let's start with how I became mired in it as a SEAL.

Behind my love for virtually all things associated with being a SEAL, there was one thing I didn't care for, specifically something called blast exposure. Simply stated, that's the term associated with being in the proximity of explosions related to demolitions, explosives of any type, and rocket or artillery fire and being exposed to the percussion that is now known to wreak havoc with the central nervous system. Something I came to know all too well.

The technical term for this type of exposure is blast overpressure (BOP), and it is known to cause cognitive changes in military personnel who experience it. That cumulative effect can be seen in gait alteration and vascular response in certain individuals with repeated sub-concussive blast exposure. Excessive BOP is thought to contribute to traumatic brain injury (TBI) and has a history of causing memory loss and sleep disorders. This hazardous exposure is especially severe for the Range Safety Officer (RSO). On average, an RSO within a SEAL Team training command can be exposed to BOP that far exceeds safety parameters. The limit is supposed to be seven to ten supervised events. I have personally done ten times the recommended number of exposures in one day just with shoulder-fired rockets when I was assigned to the training cadre at the Special Mission Unit. We were stretched thin, and I was the only RSO available to supervise the safe firing of the rockets.

I also suffered a serious training injury in 1992 after I'd been part of the assault team for five years, which only added to the effects of BOP. It happened when my team was conducting a CQC (close-quarter combat) hostage rescue training event. I was to be one of two primary entry men following an explosive breach on an exterior door on a balcony at our live-fire training facility. Me and the other operator were to rappel halfway down to a balcony and hold cover (security with weapons drawn) for the breacher who would place the charge and then rappel over the side of the balcony and detonate the charge under cover of that balcony. We would then finish the descent onto the balcony immediately following the detonation and make initial entry, clearing the way for the rest of the team to rappel down and enter.

I was in a set point position and situating myself in order to hold adequate cover from my side for the breacher. My number two was in the process of doing the same when my device failed and I smoked into the balcony below, about a fifteen-foot fall, hitting the back of my head on the railing and breaking my back. Luckily I was wearing body armor, which contained my torso and kept me from rupturing any internal organs. I was unconscious for the better part of an hour and didn't come to until I was in the emergency room of the local hospital, hooked to an EKG with an IV inserted. TBI wasn't a big thing at that point in time, and in terms of my duties as a SEAL, me being knocked unconscious wasn't as big a deal as me breaking my back.

My back healed enough for me to return to work, at least in the training cadre, and I resumed full active duty a year after the accident, throwing myself back into the process full tilt. That was 1992, and I didn't address my TBI until 2019. The PTSD resulting from the TBI hit me gradually over time. Hypervigilance, explosive anger, and mood swings, not being able to sleep or stay asleep, thoughts of suicide—the list goes on. I thought it would all go away after I retired and settled into civilian life because I was deeply disturbed and troubled by all of this shit going on in my head.

Turns out I was very wrong because it never went away. I didn't want to appear weak or as a pussy. I was a tough guy, a SEAL, and I wasn't supposed to feel this way. I was stronger and better than that. What I didn't know was that I had a problem deep in my brain caused by blast exposure and training accidents over the course of my career, and I had no control over these reactions and feelings. When I retired in 2009, part of my exit physical screening was to explore whether I had experienced a TBI due to vehicle-borne improvised explosive devices (VBIEDs) or IEDs. That's all they wanted to know. So, naturally, since I hadn't ever been hit by one of those I said no and that was that. That was as much as they wanted to know.

When I first came into the Teams, I read a book by a Vietnam-era SEAL who talked about what he went through when he got home after all the trauma he suffered, how he lost his marriage and struggled with alcohol and PTSD. My Platoon Chief was a Vietnam veteran, so I asked him about it.

My Chief proved less than sympathetic about the issue. "What a piece of shit," he said. "You don't listen to shit like that. You don't talk about it. Don't be a pussy. If you got that kind of shit in your head, get the fuck out." In other words, back then in the 1980s and for years afterward, the treatment for PTSD too often was denial. It was a phrase not to be spoken, and SEALs, both past and present, who'd suffered from it weren't acknowledged.

The list of my deployments, when lumped together, spanned nearly fifteen years and took me to Central America on the trails, respectively, of Pablo Escobar and Manuel Noriega. I was deployed off and on for a six-year stretch to the Balkans and was deployed, or just on call, for the Summer Olympic Games in 1992, 1996, and 2000, "just in case" as they say. When you're a Special Operations operator, there's a lot of "just in case." I also deployed to Africa and Iraq in my final two deployments in direct support of Operation Enduring Freedom and Operation Iraqi Freedom. And through it all, I never forgot the words of my Chief on how best to deal with issues associated with PTSD:

> *Don't be a pussy. If you got that kind of shit in your head,*
> *get the fuck out.*

The Gift that Keeps on Giving

PTSD is a disorder that causes an imbalance in the nervous system. It is a physiological or biological response to a traumatic experience, not a reflection of the mental strength, professionalism, or willpower of the trauma survivor. Understanding what PTSD is and how it occurs can help families accept a diagnosis and move forward with treatment.

The survival of our ancient ancestors depended on the speed in which they could identify a threat and be prepared to fight it or run away from it. We've inherited bodies that can perceive danger and trigger a fight-or-flight response in a split second and almost entirely subconsciously. Once that alarm goes off, a potent cocktail containing around thirty hormones and chemicals rushes into our system to get us ready to survive. In most circumstances, we metabolize this cocktail within twelve to thirty hours and go on about our lives.

Everyone has a threshold for how much of the fight-or-flight cocktail their body can tolerate without a problem. PTSD develops when an event causes the body to flood the system with more of the cocktail than it can tolerate. For example, a typical combat situation may result in ten to twelve doses of the fight-or-flight

26

cocktail within ten minutes, and that could put a service member over their body's threshold.

Once an individual has gone over their threshold, their body adapts by making changes in the nervous system's wiring. The result is a highly active system that perceives threats more often and more intensely than someone without PTSD. Therefore, trauma survivors spend a great deal of time in a fight-or-flight state, even when there is no present danger. Those who are experiencing PTSD symptoms are feeling the effects of a body that is hell-bent on their survival, akin in some respects to being engaged in constant combat.

Special Operations training builds up and reinforces that fight-or-flight in order to create an operator who can be the most effective in combat. This begs the question: What do they do to dial that down at the end?

The not so good news is that time does not heal PTSD.

It was during the tail end of this phase of my career when an incident in Coronado crystallized the reality that I was suffering from the disorder. I'd just returned from my last deployment, set to retire within a year. My wife and I were walking our dogs when a young adult male in his early twenties, along with three teenage females, were leaving the nearby Coronado High School and were walking down the street toward us to their car. They were very upset that they had lost a volleyball game, of all things. Screaming at the top of their lungs about how "Coronado sucks! Fuck you, Coronado!" On and on. We were standing right there and immediately I knew I'd had enough of this crap. Without taking my eyes off of my perceived threat, I handed our dogs' leash to my wife and started to approach this guy who was now standing half inside his vehicle and laying on his horn and still yelling at the top of his lungs.

What I didn't hear was my wife yelling at me to not do anything. "Steve! Let's just walk away!"

By now the three girls had gotten inside the car and were laughing, and the young man took serious note of me but was still laying on the horn. I tried breaking his attention, to calm him down so he'd stop doing what he was doing, but to no avail.

"Fuck you, old man!" he yelled at the top of his lungs.

Well, what's an "old man" to do? I slapped his windshield with the palm of my hand to really gain his attention. It shattered. From one end to the other, and right where I hit it looked as though I'd taken a baseball bat to it. Well, that made him stop honking the horn. The girls inside were now freaking out. He was yelling that he was calling the cops, and my wife was pulling me away from the asshole, fearing what I might do next. Lucky for me there were witnesses who came to my side when the police arrived.

I was in Condition Red, maybe even Black. I never heard my wife warning me off. I had zero sense or control of what I was doing, which wasn't normal for me.

Four local police officers arrived and peacefully defused the situation. The senior patrolman, guessing I was in the Teams, approached me and asked for my side of the story. He also asked who I was with and inquired if I had just come home. I had literally been home a week, maybe two when this happened. He took control of everything and the incident was resolved. I agreed to pay for the windshield, and the young man was let go with a written warning.

A hairpin trigger like that is a big part of PTSD. I didn't know. I never tied everything together. But the lingering effects of my TBI due to blast exposure and any number of shitty parachute landings and so on had produced a cumulative result, and it was only getting worse.

Then in 2019 I was out in New Mexico visiting my father when my PTSD struck full bore, triggered by a near traffic accident when my father narrowly avoided T-boning a truck that decided to "shoot the gap" in an intersection while we were doing fifty miles per hour. I was left deeply shaken. I'd almost been in a helicopter accident on a deployment, and I had a flashback to that moment. My dad and I were on our way to meet a member of his circle of friends for coffee. This gentleman had flown a B-52 as part of Operation Rolling Thunder in Vietnam. His aircraft got its tail blown off, but he managed to eject and spent 111 days as a prisoner of war in the Hanoi Hilton. He continued his service, got his master's in psychology before retiring, and became a counselor for the Veterans Administration specializing in PTSD. My father went to buy our coffee after telling the story of our near accident, and his friend got this serious look on his face.

"You look visibly shaken by this," he said to me. "Are you okay?"

"No, I don't think so," I told him. I still felt panicked.

As sometimes happens with PTSD, the near car accident had released all the pent-up emotions I had been holding in for years. I'd already left the Navy for good and moved with my wife from Coronado to Upstate New York to start the next phase of our lives. But I knew I was going to lose the marriage, and potentially much more, if I didn't seek help at long last.

I called my wife that day and described to her what happened.

"Are you okay?" she asked me.

"I don't think so," I told her too.

My first wife had never really gotten me, I don't think, but my second wife did. She was a retired Navy Chief herself, having served as Administrative Chief at SEAL Team 4. She also had worked at the Pentagon for the Joint Chiefs of Staff and a lot of other commands before retiring. She told me how she was always walking on eggshells with me, that she never knew how I was going to react, or overreact, to something.

I had no idea. I'd just learned to live with it, so I thought, and I believed others in my life did as well. I didn't know how to ask for help. Such a simple but also difficult thing to do. I couldn't bear the thought of losing her, especially after moving our post-military lives to the Finger Lakes Region where our property sits on one of those lakes. I knew I had to get help, to save myself as well as my marriage.

Thanks to the intervention and urging of Red, my father's POW friend, I contacted a former commanding officer I knew at Naval Special Warfare Command HQ and explained what was happening. All the crazy shit going on in my head. I'd only had the one flashback, but there were so many other things going on and I couldn't do anything about it. I felt as if I had no control.

My former CO put me in touch with a fellow retired SEAL from the Preservation of the Force and Family (POTFF) program within SOCOM, who told me about the myriad of opportunities including Home Base, an innovative regimen designed to treat warriors suffering from a multitude of issues, including PTSD.

Well, I'll tell you, Home Base saved my life. It was like a kind of twelve-step program, showing me how denial gives way to recognition. The more you acknowledge what's happening to you, the more you're able to talk about it, and the easier it gets to deal with. I've got this and this is what I'm doing to get treatment for it. It's hard to do, hard to talk about. But once you start, you get a greater understanding of what you're going through. You come to terms with it.

Initially, I spent a week as an intake patient, getting tests and speaking with the medical professionals and staff. Less than a month later, I spent another two weeks as an outpatient with a whole group of veterans going through the same stuff I was. I saw a variety of therapists at Home Base who put their finger right on what was happening to me, both mentally and physically.

As a result, I'm a hundred percent better than I was fifteen years ago. Those weeks there were equivalent to a whole year of therapy, and they saved my marriage and, very likely, myself.

When Admiral Bill McRaven was commander of all SOCOM forces, he initiated POTFF to address the issues that the operators coming back from various theaters of war and their families at home face. With a focus on improving the short- and long-term well-being of operators and their families, the program offered spiritual, psychological, and other forms of help. "We broke these guys. We need to do our best to send them back into the civilian sector as whole as possible," says a now retired SEAL captain who's very familiar with the program.

Groups such as Home Base, SOCOM Warrior Care Program, Wounded Warrior Project, Warriors at Ease, Family Readiness Group, and Veterans Affairs, as well as doctors and many other entities, can all offer help to operators who need it. The trick is getting the operators to accept it.

As a now retired SOF Command Sergeant Major said in many of his talks with fellow operators, "The point of all this therapy is, now you see your demons coming and you say, 'Good morning. How the fuck are you doing?' You don't have to embrace them. But you have to be able to say, 'Good morning,' and let them go."

With focus now more than ever on helping operators coming home from war, the hope is to see a decrease in suicides, mental health issues, and marital problems. By offering comprehensive resources and eliminating stigmas associated with seeking professional help, SOCOM commanders are hoping to provide their special operators with a better life once their career with the military is over.

What This Means for You

In essence, COVID has turned us all into special operators with our everyday lives serving as the battleground. For so many, so little remains the way it was before the pandemic struck. We are at war with an unseen enemy, and the rules of engagement continue to change. That war has beaten and battered us, left us traumatized, and has effectively caused traumatic injuries to our psyches instead of our brains.

We've lost loved ones, went months without seeing friends or elderly relatives, endured the passing of those close to us without the ability to mourn in a way that might heal the soul. So the wounds stay open, festering and rotting as the problems and the complications mount. What, though, can be done to close them?

A Prescription for Healing

It starts with taking responsibility for yourself because if you don't do that, first and foremost, you won't be able to assume responsibility for anyone, or even anything, else. We can't stop life from piling on, but we can disperse the weight by not looking for someone else to blame. That's tantamount to retreat, to giving up and giving in. Taking responsibility for your place in the New Normal is tantamount to holding your ground with the strength of resilience in the face of adversity.

- **Get help.** Open up. Don't hold it in. Do what I did when I finally acknowledged I was suffering from PTSD. You need to find your Home Base, whether that be over regular coffee with friends or therapy of some kind (even online).

- **Don't blame yourself.** You didn't cause this problem. It wasn't your fault, and it's not in your control. What *is* in your control is how you deal with it all, how you cope, how you put on a brave face no matter what level of despair you may be feeling.

- **Be positive.** That means finding small victories more than large ones. We all need to find pleasure in that which might have barely brought a smile to our faces before. The new job might come with less of a salary but more time to attend your children's games or recitals. The new home or apartment might represent a downsize, but you're still living with the people who make life worthwhile.

Airman Steve on board the USS Ranger in 1982

CHAPTER 2

Walking in Mud—Literally

I have been driven many times upon my knees by the
overwhelming conviction that I had nowhere else to go.
My own wisdom and that of all about me seemed
insufficient for that day.

—ABRAHAM LINCOLN

That quote from perhaps our greatest president is as appropriate
as any about the times in which we live now. It also captures
the humility that so characterized the man who presided over the
nation during the only other era in our history that rivals the challenges we face today.

Indeed, these times have humbled us all, made us feel smaller
and often powerless. But, as Lincoln suggests, accepting the humility that has been forced upon us all rather than fighting it makes
for a far better strategy to emerge from the mud that has bogged
us down. We are, in fact, no smaller; it's only that the challenges
thrust upon us are bigger.

The mission statement of this chapter is to help us understand
how remaining humble in the face of life's mission is the best way
to be responsible for our own fates and futures.

In Order to Lead, You Must First Follow

One of the biggest lessons I learned in the Navy was this: being a good follower, understanding the directions that I received and executing those orders properly, will lead to trust and greater responsibility. I was treated fairly and firmly by my Chiefs and officers and did my utmost to reciprocate when I was in a position of leadership. Did I always do what was expected? No. I failed at times, but I learned from my mistakes.

You do what you need to do and, sometimes, you do it because no one else wants to. You do things you'd never expected that aren't at all what you signed up for. You respond to a need, humbled in the face of a greater mission you're a part of.

Nobody asked for COVID. Before it arrived, for the most part everyone was happy. (I know I was.) We were all content—401(k)s blossoming, kids growing. Even when we saw COVID coming, we didn't think it would be as bad as it became. But our applecart was upended, flipped and dumped, with us standing there looking at the disaster with our mouths wide open in shock. We found ourselves walking in mud, in a situation we had no control over.

Frogman School

It was winter 1984 and we were Frogmen in a Frogman school. This wasn't any ordinary school for Special Operations like advanced demolition, sniper, or special intelligence. This school was learning how to pilot, navigate, repair, and maintain an underwater submersible known at the time as a Swimmer Delivery Vehicle (a.k.a. SDV, later SEAL Delivery Vehicle). The SDV, which has been in continuous operational service since 1972, is used primarily for covert or clandestine missions to denied-access areas, meaning areas either held by hostile forces or where military activity would draw notice and response.

First you need to understand that the SDV is a free-flooding submersible and the Frogmen inside ride exposed to the water, breathing from the vehicle's compressed air supply or using their own scuba gear or both in order to extend the length of the dive. The SDV program dates back to World War II, initiated by the Office of Strategic Services Maritime Unit (OSS MU) and used by a few of our allies, such as the Italians and British.

The Mark VIII (a.k.a. MK 8, or Eight Boat) SDV, the model that is still in use today, was developed and phased in to replace the Mark VII starting in 1983. A magnificent group of Frogmen and engineers get the credit for that stalwart of the SEAL community for many decades. "Gator" Parks, the godfather of SDV, especially should be hailed for the SDV program and the Mark VIII.

SDVs carry a pilot, copilot/navigator, and four-person combat swimmer team and their equipment to and from maritime mission objectives on land or at sea. The pilot and copilot can be a part of the fighting team if the mission dictates. The SDV can deliver four fully equipped SEALs to the mission area, be "parked" or loiter in the area, retrieve the operators, and then return to the launch site.

The crew and passenger compartment in the Mark VIII is small, cramped, and pitch black except for the dim lights of the instrument panel; operators describe riding in an SDV as like "being locked in a little black coffin deep under the water." As such, many SEALs are hesitant to operate out of an SDV or seek orders there, and only about 10 percent at any one time are qualified to operate in one.

I didn't volunteer to be assigned to SDVs. Most of us didn't enter BUD/S to go into that particular line of work in the Teams, but nonetheless, I got there and I embraced the suck. Remind you of anything yet?

We learned the intricacies of the SDV, the maintenance, repair, and the concept of the optimal dive profile, and we took our turns in the barrel first in the simulator and then in the boats themselves.

I say "boats" because at the time there were two models in use in the Teams, the Mark VIII and the Mark IX. To put it succinctly about the variance between these two crafts, imagine you're in Drivers Education and there are two cars to learn in. One is an SUV—steady, lumbering, and not very sporty but can carry your friends and gear. The other is a Corvette—responsive, faster, and if you're not careful, you'll kill yourself and your passenger with a cargo space the size of a sports car's trunk.

I did the best I could, as did my classmates of fellow Frogs. We laughed, we yelled in frustration, but we finally succeeded in learning the basics of these two machines in a twelve-week course.

We all were assigned dive buddies but also rotated to see who matched best. One of the things I learned in the Teams was that an intricate understanding of your dive buddy was just as important as the same for your gear. If you had a dive buddy who you clicked with, it was pure magic. If you didn't, disaster was right around every corner.

My dive buddy Max and I were good friends and roommates from BUD/S. He was great—a quiet demeanor and our BUD/S class unofficial "gray man" but who could make everyone laugh just by giving a funny look or mild reaction.

In SDV school, he and I were paired up for our Final Training Exercise (FTX) dive. We had worked together in the past on several dives and clicked. When I saw our pairing, I thought, "Okay, me and Max. We can do this!" Not so sure he felt the same, but we had to do it. Looking back now, I think the training cadre were bored with the exceptional performance of everyone else and they wanted a memorable dive that they could laugh about for years. Max and I didn't fail to disappoint anyone in that respect.

The mission: Dive our Mark IX, the Nine Boat, the Corvette, within the confines of San Diego Bay first by passing through the gauntlet of the Coronado Bridge pilings to the near area of Spanish Landing in the north of the bay. Surface briefly for a thumbs-up from the safety boat. Make a U-turn and head south back through the gauntlet of the bridge and continue to the Emory Channel area just south of the Coronado Cays where there used to be a bunch of moored sailboats.

We were to "bottom out and anchor" the SDV, swim via combat swimmer mode to a cache that we would locate by using a handheld underwater location device, retrieve the cache from a tethered buoy, and return to our SDV via the same manner but using a different frequency of pinger, special for the boat, so we wouldn't swim in circles and never find it. We would then navigate our way back to the pier at NAB Coronado and debrief. This was all set to take place entirely at night. Anticipated dive time was about four and five hours.

Once the dive gear and SDV were prepped, we briefed our plan, covered contingencies, and then "jocked up" for our dive. As we were getting ready, Max pulled me aside and confided that he was tone deaf to the frequencies of the pinger devices, so him using the locator would be of no use. I said, "No worries, I can do that part. I'm pretty good with it."

The dive started off great. We got underway and headed to the Spanish Landing area in the north of the bay via the gauntlet. The part about the bridge is very important to note here because SDV students historically have clipped, scraped, or flat-out T-boned the underwater bridge pilings. These things were mammoth, and if you were cruising at full speed in an SDV, you could really cause some horrific damage to the boat and even yourself and your dive buddy.

The navigator's job in the SDV was to do just that: navigate. He used various knobs on his screen to adjust the gain and filter out clutter so he could see the real dangers and navigate the pilot around those hazards. A really good navigator could pick out buoy chains and count pier pilings like they were trees along a rural freeway.

We threaded that needle, hit our exact checkpoint at the north end, and then surfaced briefly to get a thumbs-up from our instructor (who tonight was Senior Chief "Vie") in the safety boat so we could continue. Man, we were smokin' it. We got through the gauntlet again on our way south and things were going as planned. Hell, better than planned! We arrived at our bottom-out point without issue.

This is where things got wonky.

Max and I prepped the boat for our next part of the mission, the combat swimmer leg. Electronics off? Check. Unplug underwater communications from full face mask? Check. Turn on boat pinger? Check. Outside of the SDV we connected our buddy line, checked to make sure it was secured, and then set the anchor to the SDV so it wouldn't drift off.

I slipped the earpiece of the handheld pinger receiver under my wetsuit hood and over my ear and tuned it to the appropriate frequency. Then I squeezed Max on the arm to signal I was ready to go, and I got the squeeze back signaling he was just as ready. Two Frogmen, underwater and swimming to retrieve our secret cache. Right out of the action thriller books.

It's dark as a closet. Max is backing me up with the swimmer "attack board," keeping our time and distance and monitoring our depth. An attack board is a handheld platform, about eight by ten feet, that has attached to it a dimly illuminated compass for direction, a depth gauge to maintain a constant safe depth, and a watch to measure your time for each "leg." In this case our leg was a straight shot to the cache from the SDV but in shallower water about a hundred yards away from where we'd parked the SDV. Bottom line is the attack board allows combat swimmers to accurately navigate underwater.

We reached the cache without incident. *Bam! Take that! We're cool, baby.* We proceeded to disconnect the cache from the buoy line in the dark, silty mud at the bottom of the bay. The cache was a C-4 haversack, clipped to the line with a carabiner.

"Oh...my...God!" I'm thinking. "This thing is heavy as hell!" I'm standing there in the mud and silt looking at Max and wondering how we're both supposed to swim this, use the attack board to navigate our reciprocal heading back to the boat, and then rely upon the handheld receiver to actually zero in on the SDV once we're in its vicinity. Max had the attack board so he couldn't swim this beast, which left me to lug it, pissing me off to no end. "They're probably up there laughing their asses off at us" was my thought.

I tried swimming it horizontal, but it just laid me down in the mud. So, now what? We couldn't just leave the cache on the bottom; that would be mission failure, and quitting. So, I slung the heavy haversack over my shoulder and literally started walking on the bottom of San Diego Bay, high-stepping with fins in the mud and silt and using the receiver to locate the pinger in our boat to lead us back. Max was using the attack board to keep us on heading in the direction of the boat, which he got the reciprocal heading for on the way to the cache. He was swimming just at my head level at about fifteen-foot depth.

Each stride I took with the fins on in the mud got harder as we slogged our way to the SDV. It felt like I was back in BUD/S swimming against the rip current on a two-mile ocean swim. Us, heading in one direction while an unseen "thing" wants to push us another way. A rip current is a strong, localized, and narrow stream of water that moves directly away from the shore, cutting through the lines of breaking waves like a river running out to sea. It's strongest and fastest nearest the surface of the water and will push a swimmer out to sea in a heartbeat.

This was me and Max, hauling the haversack with the clump, our proverbial rip current, making our way to our SDV through silt, mud, the outgoing tide, and the dark ocean.

At this point I think it's important to fill you in on what the "clump" was. It was a square block of lead with an eyebolt going through it, for the purpose of tying a line to it. In the Teams we melted these blocks of lead down and poured the molten stuff into forms for our dive weights that we wore on a waist belt to help us stay below the surface of the water. This particular clump weighed about forty pounds. What we were supposed to do was remove the clump from the haversack, clip it onto the buoy line, and lug the haversack back to the SDV.

We made it back to the SDV, opened the back hatch of the Nine Boat, loaded the heavy cache into the back, and secured it. By now I'd realized we were supposed to leave the lead clump there, at the cache site, reattaching it to the buoy line, and take only the haversack back with us. Damn it! At this point, we had no choice but to lug the clump with us back to the finish, pier side. We then did everything in reverse as when we'd arrived: pulled the anchor, disconnected the buddy line, climbed into the boat, and plugged in comms, turning everything on and getting underway. Max and I survived the dive and passed our final test for school, but not without a good ass chewing by the Senior Chief for not paying attention and failing to get things right from the get-go.

What This Means for You

These times require all of us, quite literally, to find the smoothest waters to operate. Get ourselves out of the mud and away from the rip current. In Greek mythology, there's the famous story of Sisyphus, banished to the underworld by the god Zeus who forces him to roll a boulder up a hill for eternity. Every time he nears the top of the hill, the boulder rolls back down.

There are times these days when we all feel like Sisyphus, pushing that boulder up a hill or, like me, walking in mud in the bottom of a dark bay, feeling the current push against you. The trick is this: stay calm and remember to breathe and to keep moving forward. Don't let the boulder crush you under its weight any more than I did with the forty-pound clump of lead attached to the haversack as I slogged along the ocean floor.

"The world breaks everyone," Ernest Hemingway once wrote, "and afterward many are strong at the broken places."

The world will break you only if you let it. While we stand humbled before it, we can be strong without breaking. Humility doesn't mean accepting defeat. It doesn't mean cowering in the face of your enemy. It means accepting and acknowledging the power of the enemy and that enemy's capacity to adversely affect your life. Remaining humble in the face of that makes successfully negotiating the New Normal a far easier task.

A Prescription for Healing

- **Know where you're going.** You may have heard the Ralph Waldo Emerson quote, "It's not the destination, it's the journey." In this case it's both. Chart your journey with the wind and the currents as much as possible. It'll take time to reach your destination, but you'll get there.

- **Raise yourself up.** If a man as great as Abraham Lincoln can be driven to his knees, there's no shame in finding yourself there. You won't be measured by being down so much as how quickly and firmly you rise up again. As Vince Lombardi once famously said, "The greatest achievement lies not in rising, but in rising again after you've fallen."

- **Be humble.** This, above all else, is a time for humility and accepting the fact that events are no more yours to control than the currents of the ocean. Find strength in that acknowledgment and keep walking through the mud until you're on solid ground again. "If you're going through hell," Winston Churchill once said, "keep going."

LEADERSHIP

BUD/S Third Phase on San Clemente Island, 1983 (Steve is third from the left in the front row)

CHAPTER 3

The Bitter End

Here's to cheating, stealing, fighting, and drinking. If you cheat, may you cheat death. If you steal, may you steal a woman's heart. If you fight, may you fight for a brother.

—IRISH TOAST
(Dedicated to Jody Mac, a true warrior, operator, and friend)

Hard times call for leaders; in fact, hard times can help *create* leaders. Finding the right leader, or becoming one yourself, makes for a keen strategy to get out of the mud. Either you will follow someone out who knows the way, or you will lead others out by charting your own course.

I guess the overriding point I'm making here is that this isn't a time to go it alone. Indeed, when it comes to walking in mud, we fail alone and succeed together through the power of our common humanity. That was the subtitle of another book in which I was featured (*Overcoming: Lessons in Overcoming Adversity and the Power of Our Common Humanity*). That book's author, the esteemed African American orthopedic surgeon Dr. Augustus White, says it this way:

We are all so much more similar than different. As an orthopedic surgeon, I can tell you that when you make the incision, when you look inside, everybody is the same. Open up the skin and underneath it's all one. The reality of the body tells you this. It's a reality doctors see constantly. Our humanness is greater than our cultural differences, our differences in status or rank, our racial differences. In the final analysis we're just human and now we need the power of our common humanity to help us spot a future through the clouds, to bring light to the darkness that threatens to consume us.

"Pandemics will always be characterized by their randomness, pitilessness, and power to sicken and kill," Jeffrey Kluger wrote for *Time* in February of 2020. "The human response, when it's at its best, is defined by collective courage and compassion, a 'not-on-our-watch' refusal to let a disease have its way with our fellow humans. And to limit the impact of—and ultimately defeat—the current coronavirus pandemic, that's exactly what we'll need."

And that's where leadership comes in. The mission statement for this chapter is to demonstrate how leadership plays an enhanced role in the New Normal.

The Forever Deployment

"The only courage that matters," wrote author and journalist Mignon McLaughlin, "is the kind that gets you from one moment to the next."

Life in the military, especially the US military, requires you to be prepared to deploy wherever and whenever the chain of command dictates and for how long.

The COVID-19 pandemic was sort of like that yesteryear deployment of our fathers' and grandfathers' wars, except you have your spouse and kids with you and hopefully, if you weren't furloughed or altogether let go, you worked from home. Working from home was probably a very new concept for many and not as easy to master as most might think. At first, I'm sure many thought it would be fun. Getting to hang out with the family all while doing your job from the makeshift office converted from the living room or basement just for you and maybe your spouse.

Now enter the distractions, the inability to maintain a steady workflow, the interruptions. If both spouses are working from home and there are kids that need to be schooled, it can get very daunting. If you nailed it and had no issues, great! For those eager to get back to the office because the kids are killing the "flow" and your spouse continues to interrupt or you're both competing for maximum internet bandwidth, I am truly sorry. You must feel as though you're on that forever deployment. You may be at your bitter end, stretched to the absolute limit.

What, though, does the "bitter end" mean exactly? The dictionary defines it as (1) the conclusion of a difficult or unpleasant situation, (2) the last or furthest extremity, (3) in nautical terms, the inboard end of an anchor chain, line, or cable, and (4) to the limit of one's efforts, to the last extremity.

In 2003, while serving as the Command Master Chief of a Team at Little Creek, I was deployed as the senior enlisted of a 120+ person Special Operations Joint Task Force (SOJTF) operating off the Horn of Africa. Somalia, to be more specific. The bitter end of Northeast Africa, to put it plainly. Some would argue that it sometimes feels like the bitter end of the world.

We deployed with folks from our Team, our sister Team, and some extremely expensive assets—a submarine and our SDVs, along with a lot of other classified equipment. We were initially based out of Camp Lemonnier in Djibouti for phase one of the operation. The camp, which was originally established as a garrison for the French Foreign Legion and named for a French army general, was located at the opposite side of Djibouti-Ambouli International Airport. The base was leased by Djibouti to the

United States in 2001 following the terrorist attacks on 9/11, and the United States started staging counterterrorism missions in that region from the camp.

At that time, it was a somewhat austere camp and was populated mostly with Marines and Air Force personnel along with some Army and Navy, primarily in direct support of the overall US mission and the Special Operations mission in the new Global War on Terrorism, or GWOT. Within the main camp was another camp. Fenced off to nonessential base personnel, it headquartered the SOF Crisis Response Element, or CRE. Within that fence were Army Special Forces, Air Force Special Operations, and Naval Special Warfare personnel, together with a SEAL platoon and Special Warfare Combatant-Craft Crewman (SWCC) detachment. There were also Navy EOD who were in direct support of the CRE but also part of the overall de-mining mission for the area.

Inside that camp within a camp was a specific berthing area for the operators that was located near the farthest quadrant of the overall camp closest to the shores of Djibouti, where you could almost smell Somalia. This was the bitter end. And it was there on my first night in the country I was invited by my friend and the SEAL Platoon Chief "Big Daddy" to partake in some sanctioned beers in an almost *M*A*S*H*-like scene at a hut aptly named the Bitter End. As we stood outside and sipped our Coronas, we got caught up on our respective lives, and Big Daddy told me about the platoon he was leading and his personal challenges of taking them out of Iraq and finishing the deployment in this unknown mission, in a place none of them had ever deployed to prior.

The first month our task force was there we coexisted alongside the SEAL platoon, a Special Forces Operational Detachment Alpha (ODA) team, and some other SOF folks. As I said, the aforementioned were specifically there for the CRE mission for that region, but some, though not all, were also part of our planning for phase two of our operation. Since Big Daddy's platoon had just been pulled out of Iraq after three months of combat and would rotate home after three more months in the Horn of Africa, we wouldn't be bringing them along. We would pick up the incoming SEAL platoon that was due to replace Big Daddy's. The SF team was waiting to rotate into Afghanistan after their CRE rotation and go home from there, but they would join us for phase two as our airborne Quick Reaction Force, or QRF.

The base commander, a one-star Marine general, was well aware of the Bitter End's existence and sanctioned it because there was already a club of sorts on the main side of the camp. This distanced the SOF personnel from the others and allowed everyone to enjoy themselves and relax without the edge of rivalry and the occasional brawl, not to mention "loose lips sinking ships," a.k.a. the need to maintain operational security (OPSEC).

The commanding general and his Senior Enlisted Advisor occasionally made an appearance at the Bitter End and mingled among everyone there while enjoying a beer or two. The one major rule was no getting out of control. Big boy rules. Sure, people might have had too much at times, but I didn't see anyone out-of-control drunk. It was a mellow scene—people just talking, socializing, and getting familiar with who they were working with in a not so starched environment. A few hours of R&R.

We would hang out there on occasion just to get acquainted with the people who would be joining us on the ship for the second phase of the operation. Some attached to our task force were only there for the planning portion, phase one, like then Lieutenant JG Michael Murphy, posthumous Medal of Honor recipient from Afghanistan whose tragic passing was chronicled in the film *Lone Survivor*, from the book of the same title by Marcus Luttrell.

We knew him as "Murph," but he had another nickname that he earned there at Camp Lemonnier. When Murph first checked in and he was getting his security badge for the secure portion of the compound, the newly arrived Army staffer who was issuing the badges hadn't come across any Navy people before. She thought his writing was sloppy and that "Ltjg" was really "Lt J6" so she just typed Lt J6 on his ID badge. So Murph's new nickname then became J6.

This was a great group of people we assembled for this special mission. From the operations planning staff to the operators in the water, in the air, and on the ground who would be doing the actual missions, they were all good.

One Team, One Fight

For the second phase of the operation, we would embark aboard a Navy ship: the USS *Ogden*, at the time the oldest ship in the fleet and the last to boast an all-male crew. The ship's Command Master Chief (CMC) took a lot of pride in that fact, and he made sure to let me know when our two leaderships met for the first time for a grip and grin and coordination meeting. As he and I were walking around the ship, I tried as best I could to subtly inform him that we would be bringing two enlisted females aboard as part of the task force. He was beside himself. Meanwhile, my CO was doing the same with the ship's CO, who objected to the entire notion, stating plainly that his strong preference was for us to not bring the women aboard. He inquired if we could do without them, but eventually he came around and seemed to take it in stride as part of this already new and different mission.

When we embarked aboard the ship, everyone was given their berthing assignments and the two females were given a stateroom to share in Officers Country. The SEAL platoon and SF ODA were assigned the Marine berthing, and the E-7 and above battle staff were given similar and appropriate berthing as well.

I guess because my CO and I refused to leave the two females behind, I was given the worst bunk assignment in the Chiefs' berthing. I would have to get on all fours to roll in and out of my rack. I was also located in the loudest section of the berthing compartment, the HVAC piping, which hummed constantly. On occasion, I would be woken up on non-mission nights with my rack curtains flying open and a flashlight in my face "by mistake" by an individual purportedly looking for someone else for the next watch. Seemed the "mistake" always happened around 2:00 a.m.

Oh well. Not like they could screw up my sleep any more than what I was already experiencing, despite their best efforts.

Within the Chiefs' mess, the Task Force Senior Enlisted (E-7 and above) were ostracized to a degree and made out to be a disruption to what was supposed to be a routine deployment for the ship's crew. Granted, we had displaced the Marines on board, who had been sent to Camp Lemonnier for the duration of our operation. And we'd also forced our hand with regard to the females coming aboard, so the "one team, one fight" concept was going to be a challenge to achieve.

We persevered despite the small challenges we put before the ship's leadership. The ship's CO seemed to be okay, whereas the CMC refused to speak with me about anything other than official business; you know, the important things such as SEAL and SF guys not wearing shirts while working out. We did the absolute best we could given the circumstances we were all in.

Leadership challenges popped up frequently, and certain issues had to be addressed as a group. We had our own issues with the ship's crew wanting to take pictures, get cozy with the two females, and touch the gear we used, which the CO and I brought up to the ship's leadership, part and parcel of what most times were unnecessary distractions.

Combating boredom between the missions wasn't too much of a challenge since there were only a few days between each, thanks to the Task Force CO and Operations shop doing phenomenal work coordinating the operations side of things.

Coordinating an operation from the ship—in addition to the submarine, overhead assets for "eye in the sky" intelligence, surveillance and reconnaissance, and occasional gunship support—would be considered a hat trick. The QRF comprised two SBT detachments, a SEAL platoon, an SF ODA, and a Navy helicopter detachment specially equipped for combat operations, i.e., Hellfire missiles and door gunners, all to protect the SDV operators and the reconnaissance team going ashore. All that for ultimately six guys doing some "sneaking, peeking, and leaving a gift."

Our task force was, in total, more than 120 personnel from several organizations, all brought together to conduct an operation, the likes of which had never been undertaken before. It was a proof-of-concept operation that would get used again and again over the next decade or so. Despite all the obstacles we had to overcome and setbacks we encountered, we established a template for a new brand of military operation.

What This Means for You

The previously obscure terms "the bitter end" and "forever deployment" are uniquely suited to address the New Normal that finds us walking in mud. Indeed, many of us have reached our own bitter end these past two years or so and feel as if we've been on one of those forever deployments with no defined end.

COVID-19, along with the economic and social stress it has produced, has left us mired in uncertainty over where we go from here. The virus has returned in a mutated form as of this writing, leaving us with even more uncertainty. Will the vaccines work in the long term or just the short? Will I lose my job and, if so, how will I get another? What about the lingering effects of social isolation, particularly on children and especially teenagers? How do I navigate the New Normal of the workplace? Will working from home be a forever part of that new workplace normal?

Questions without answers, thanks to the only certainty being uncertainty. But here's the thing: like it was for us on the USS *Ogden*, we're all in this together exploring new ground and charting new territory. My experiences on that deployment weren't the first or last time I was involved in something that had never been tried before. We encountered our bumps in the road along the way, but we ultimately got to the end because of the strength of our leadership, teamwork, and remaining steadfast to our principles.

Those are the same attributes we need to rely on during the forever deployment we all find ourselves on now. We've reached our proverbial "bitter end" of this thing called COVID-19 and the horrific period it dominated, taking up virtually all of 2020 and spilling over well into 2021. It's going to take leadership and teamwork to emerge whole and strong on the other side.

Times of stress bring out the worst in some and the best in others. The best is adopting the kind of warrior mentality reflective of being mired in a forever deployment. The worst is adopting an attitude aptly referred to as "the Disease of Me." George Stillman Hillard offered the most appropriate definition of that when he said, "The force of selfishness is as inevitable and as calculable as the force of gravitation."

Pat Riley, professional basketball executive for the Miami Heat and a former championship coach and player in the NBA, argues that whether we know it or not, all of us are team players, and it is through the team that we find significance. Yet the team can be undermined by the Disease of Me. In his book *The Winner Within*, he describes it as the overpowering belief in the importance of oneself.

"The most difficult thing for individuals to do when they're part of the team is to sacrifice," he writes. "It is so easy to become selfish in a team environment."

Just as sacrifice is a vital part of leadership, as much as setting the proper example, selfishness represents the antithesis of leadership.

Feeling and bearing a responsibility for others, as opposed to yourself, is one of the best formulas of all to lift us from the forever deployment in which we find ourselves. Getting back to the notion of common humanity, the best way to lift yourself is to focus on lifting others as well. Accepting and welcoming more responsibility, a crucial criterion of leadership, can be stunningly effective in yanking you from the chaos so many of us have settled into.

Put another way: think like a warrior and decide how you're going to win not just the battle but the war as well.

A Prescription for Healing

Okay, so we talked about the importance of sacrifice as opposed to selflessness. With that in mind, here are the big three mission-critical actions to help you lead yourself and others out of the mud.

- **Buy in.** Leaders must redefine what the mission is and why it is so vital. First and foremost, we must recommunicate why what we do is so important to the world and to each of us. Creating that buy-in is paramount. Post-pandemic, getting people to commit to safety is going to be equally crucial and vital to the notion of buying in, as is recognizing the New Normal may have stark differences with the old. That means leaders have to step up as guides to steer others, whether they be family members, business associates, employees, or friends, along the new path many of us will find ourselves negotiating.

- **Have purpose.** Leaders must make their people know why they are so critical to the mission. We all need connection. Individuals want to know how they are critical to the effort. They need to know the answers to, "Why do I need to be here? Why am I so valuable?" People want to be wanted and want to know their role and purpose. In the New Normal, though, that role and purpose may well have changed, placing an even greater responsibility on leaders to make this new landscape their own so those enlisted in their charge feel the game may have changed but the rules remain the same. As Jeff Boss wrote for *Forbes* in October of 2016, in an article titled "3 Ways to See Opportunity When Others See Crisis," "All it takes sometimes to move from being stuck to unstuck is a willingness to face difficult questions; to move out of your own way because, more often than not, how you see the problem oftentimes is the problem."

- **Listen.** Leaders must address concerns and fears head-on, recognizing the fact that your people want to know they'll be heard. Great organizations, from the largest to the smallest, and great leaders will gather their people's concerns, address each one, and show how they will handle them and mitigate the risk to their people. "We know many of you are concerned about X and this is how we're going to ensure that each of you gets Z," or "Here is how and what we will be doing to aggressively help solve those problems..." At its base level, life is about getting from point A to point B, a simplicity we took for granted until the New Normal stripped it from us. Leaders chart the new path, the new way to get from A to B, whether it be for their family, civic organization, neighborhood, or business. As Steven Covey, author of *7 Habits of Highly Successful People*, has written, "There are three constants in life...change, choice, and principles."

PRIDE

*FNGs & Training Cadre for Advanced Operator Training in 1984
(Steve is centered in the back row)*

CHAPTER 4

The Standard We Hold Ourselves To

When people kill themselves, they think they're ending the pain, but all they're doing is passing it on to those they leave behind.

—JEANNETTE WALLS

This could be any SOF operator, but it happens to be a decorated Navy SEAL operator, a breacher, who was regularly exposed to blast overpressure (BOP), or blast exposure, throughout his ten years of service. Struggling with the psychological effects of serving in four combat tours and an undiagnosed brain injury, he died by suicide on a Sunday morning in 2017 dressed in a SEAL Team shirt with the medals he earned in service next to him.

"He died from combat injuries, just not right away," his father said.

His repeated exposure to BOP severely damaged his brain by causing microscopic tears in the tissue, internal lining, and blood vessels. The SEAL told his father in the months before his death that he wanted his brain to be donated to TBI research. The SEAL's brain

61

was examined at Walter Reed National Military Medical Center, where a doctor discovered, postmortem, that he had a severe level of microscopic brain injury that was uniquely related to blast exposure, comparable to what I experienced as chronicled in chapter one.

This SEAL was far from alone.

There was a young actor who joined the Army and became a Green Beret at the age of thirty-five. He'd played college hockey and starred in a movie about the 1980 US Olympic hockey team's "Miracle on Ice" win. The film was called *Miracle*. But there was no miracle in this Green Beret's life. He died on a Monday of a self-inflicted gunshot wound.

He made it through the grueling Army Special Operations Command Green Beret training at Fort Bragg and specialized as a Special Forces Communications Sergeant, an "Eighteen Echo" or 18E operator. After training he was assigned to the 1st Special Forces Group, based at Joint Base Lewis-McChord, Washington. It was said by his teammates that he had a passionate love for his family.

He deployed in direct support of Operation Inherent Resolve, the US fight against ISIS, in 2016, according to his Army Special Operations Command records. He was a decorated warrior who came home a changed man from his experience on that deployment.

Then there was this hero, another Green Beret. The enemy could never break him, but what this decorated soldier eventually found was that his enemy was within.

Friends who served with him say he was the real Captain America. He served six tours in Afghanistan with the 82nd Airborne and the 75th Ranger regiment and a half dozen more combat tours overseas. He became a decorated Green Beret and a Silver Star recipient. He had just moved to Washington, DC, to start a coveted job at the Pentagon. Two days after America's celebration of Independence, the Fourth of July (also on a Monday night), after having dinner with his former battalion commander, he returned home and died by suicide in front of his wife.

He never got over his tour in Afghanistan in 2009 with the 2-508, a battalion that had one of the highest casualty rates of any unit during the war. That deployment was like "being in the ring with Mike Tyson for a year," according to the battalion's former Command Sergeant Major (CSM). He had a wife and two children that he loved deeply and tragically left behind.

While these men were the best of the best, they are hardly alone in the trauma that followed them home. An estimated twenty veterans take their lives every single day. We think of them as disciplined, grounded, loyal, faithful. We think of them as heroes, but their experience has left them vulnerable.

And now, thanks to this war we've all been fighting against COVID-19, we're all vulnerable. Many of us are teetering on an uneasy edge, in danger of slipping off. We may have lost our jobs, our homes, even loved ones to the pandemic. It's the very definition of life piling on.

Pride too often keeps us suffering in a box. We don't want to admit we're weak, that we're flawed. When you're a special operator on a mission, you can't show weakness. And when you're a father, a husband, or a friend, you don't want to show weakness either. That's the bad side of pride.

The good side of pride is that it makes us want to endure, to persevere, and to succeed. But having pride in success isn't about denying your vulnerability; it's about accepting it. And the mission statement of this chapter is to show you how to do that in these most challenging times when our pride is being tested along with everything else.

Suicide Hits Home

My personal experience with the act of suicide goes back to when I was four years old. People say that was too young to remember anything like that, but I'll disagree. Others say that experiencing a traumatic event when very young etches that memory into the recesses of the person's brain. It was 1967 and we were at the swim club, the Thunderbird Swim Gym, on the southwest side of Albuquerque. It was May and already a hot, high desert day. My grandfather was living with us at the time, having moved in after my grandmother died. My father converted our garage to a den/ bedroom just off our kitchen on the opposite side of the house from our living room. As my father would explain to me much later in life, my grandfather was troubled and a functioning alcoholic.

Before her death, while my grandfather would be getting ready for work, my grandmother would dutifully bring him a shot of whiskey and coffee. That was breakfast. He was an engineer working at Sandia Labs on the base. He moved his family to Albuquerque in the 1940s from the Midwest, and that's pretty much where they stayed.

On that fateful hot desert day, I remember my mother asking my grandfather if he wanted to go with us, just to get him out of the house. In his usual grumpy voice, I remember him growling, "No." I think she did it to let him know he was loved and included in whatever we did as a family. The same went for when we went to church on Sundays; she made sure to ask him if he wanted to join us.

I used to run into his room and ask him to tie my shoes for me before we went anywhere. I liked having him help me and thought it was funny when he would grumble, "When are you going to learn to tie your own shoes?" I reminded him I was only four. I would also make a point of being the first one inside the house when we would return home from someplace and race back to his room to tell him all about it.

I don't really recall the day at the big pool. My father said we went there often because it was new, and my parents wanted us to have this special experience and also to teach us to swim and just spend time together as a family. We left after a fun-filled day and journeyed back across town.

As usual, I raced inside to see my grandfather. That's when I found him. At first, I thought he had fallen asleep in his chair. Then all hell broke loose when my mother walked in. Chaos erupted. My father ran in and swept me up in his arms and rushed me out of the room. I was confused, startled.

I could hear my mother wailing and screaming. My father was now in damage-control mode. He called emergency services. The police and an ambulance showed up. Our babysitter was called to the house to come and walk my brother, sister, and me somewhere, anywhere. A neighbor was there in short order to help my dad control the storm. My dad most likely knew the policeman that showed up, since he was one himself and it was a relatively small force at the time.

That was it. My grandfather had committed suicide with his .38 revolver. Things were never the same again in our house.

The Cold Hard Facts

Depression has a myriad of causes, not the least of which is on display every day for all of us to see. I speak of pride, specifically wanting to be the best husband, father, friend, provider, boss, employee, or fill in the blank you can be. Through no fault of our own, our lives thanks to COVID and the political divisions the virus helped spawn have been so deconstructed financially and emotionally as to leave our pride wounded at the very least. Just take a look at the endless rows of cars lined up at food banks and then look for all the BMWs, Volvos, and high-end SUVs.

We've already seen a steady rise in deaths by suicide over the past two decades, and a new report by the Well Being Trust released last month found that seventy-five thousand additional people could die from what they called "deaths of despair" (which include suicide and substance use) because of COVID-19.

The physical symptoms of the novel coronavirus have been well reported for months, but it's the handful of psychological and sociological factors that are just starting to ring alarm bells. The combination of physical distancing, economic stress, barriers to mental health treatment, pervasive national anxiety, and a spike in gun sales are creating what JAMA: The Journal of the American Medical Association referred to as "a perfect storm" for suicide mortality.

Taking that a step further, a recent study undertaken by Boston University, as reported in the Medical News Today newsletter, found that "US cases of depression have tripled during the COVID-19 pandemic. Researchers estimate that more than 1 in 4 U.S. adults now report experiencing symptoms of depression. Before the pandemic, 8.5% of U.S. adults reported being depressed. That number has risen to 27.8% as the country struggles with COVID-19."

"Depression in the general population after prior large-scale traumatic events has been observed to, at most, double," notes Professor Sandro Galea, a dean at Boston University School of Public Health and a senior author of the study.

"While reports of depression have increased in response to earlier crises," the article in Medical News Today continues, "such as the 9/11 attack and the spread of Ebola in West Africa, the extent of this recent finding is something new."

Psychologist James Pennebaker of the University of Texas added this in Scientific American in December of 2020:

"Unlike any other disaster that I've studied, people are actively less close to friends and community. This is not 9/11 or an earthquake, where something big happens, and we all get back to normal pretty quickly."

People have lost jobs, careers. They can't pay the rent, can't pay the mortgage, can't provide for their kids. The simplest, most basic responsibilities have become grueling and arduous. Through no fault of our own, it makes us feel like failures because we are unable to fulfill our most basic tasks. Our pride is threatened, stripped away. We can't look our children or ourselves in the face.

"My pride has gone. We're pretty much homeless now," Omar Lightner told BBC News, also in December of 2020. "We've got two hundred bucks saved up, it's going to get us nowhere, it's the timing, it's the holidays. I sit up at night thinking how I can explain to my kids they can't have a Christmas because we have to get out of here in a few days."

Heartbreaking and made even worse by the fact that this is part and parcel of a second pandemic directly associated with COVID-19, one that targets self-esteem and self-respect, making us feel small and helpless.

Lessons from the Military

What we haven't seen quantified yet is what many experts expect to see—a staggering rise in suicides as a result of COVID. This is nothing new, regrettably, among the military community. Rising suicide rates among service members and veterans over the past decade have raised public and professional concerns. Suicide is the second leading cause of death in the US military.

Special Operations units saw twenty-two deaths by suicide in 2018, almost triple the eight cases in 2017. Even as leaders struggle to search for answers, SOCOM is acting to address the problem, instituting training and raising awareness. Commanders in other services are also addressing the issue with unusual frankness to raise awareness, an effort they hope will lower the toll and help their personnel.

The devastating scourge of suicide continues even after troops leave service, hitting the veteran community exceptionally hard. The good news for my community, and something we can learn from, is that SOCOM is working with researchers to understand underlying thought processes that lead to suicide and what actions can be taken to mitigate that behavior. Special Operations Command is also moving to address the problem by developing training to help troops recognize warning signs and teach them how to respond.

And here's more of that good news. SOF unit commanders believe a key component of mental health is promoting productive behaviors through engaged, compassionate leadership. They also believe working with family members is vital because they are often the first to see a change in behavior. The training is heavily based in cognitive behavior therapy and is designed to provide benefit to any participant regardless of their risk for suicide due to experiencing the kind of crises so many of us are dealing with as a result of COVID.

What This Means for You

The heightened stress and anxiety levels associated with the pandemic have turned us all into figurative commandos, fighting an enemy we can't see that is determined to destroy our lives, even kill us. This enemy attacks not only our bodies but also our psyches, our self-esteem, and our pride because of how it makes us feel weak, helpless, and ineffectual. Having no idea what tomorrow might bring and trying to make do, sometimes, on a minimum to survive.

This isn't what we signed up for. It caught us by surprise. Like special operators, we hold ourselves to a high standard, and for many of us that is a standard we are no longer able to uphold.

"Whether you've been living alone or have lost touch with friends and family, or have been furloughed or lost your job," reads a report in *IOSH*, a magazine devoted to safety, health, and well-being in the workplace, "this pandemic has left people with a battered ego and low self-esteem. COVID-19 has created a perfect storm of vulnerabilities huge numbers of people have been ill-prepared to manage."

Dhara Shah, a lifestyle coach and owner of Ripple Touch, put it this way in the same article: "I've seen people turning to drinking more. You get some people who are feeling withdrawn and nervous with the concept of going out, or just generally feeling more anxious or stressed. It's increasing the strain on relationships. You get parents blocking out their own feelings to be strong for their kids. It's the struggle with the change in lifestyle as well. Loneliness has increased. Some are looking to social media for validation or reassurance and this can have the opposite effect, it can impact you negatively."

A Prescription for Healing

Shah recommends the following tips for walking in this particular mud and recovering our pride:

- **Identify negative self-talk.** Spot situations when you question yourself the most—it can help you to anticipate and prepare.

- **Check in with yourself.** Stopping and pausing, being mindful of what's on your mind and how you're feeling, can help you to turn it around.

- **Listen to what you're saying to yourself.** Don't ignore it. Hear it and make a note, as if you were keeping a journal.

- **Challenge what you're telling yourself.** Is there any fact to this? What would I be telling a friend in a similar situation? Can I do anything to change what I'm feeling bad about?

- **Talk yourself up.** Choose to acknowledge yourself, celebrate, compliment, forgive, and encourage yourself. It will feel uncomfortable at first, frustrating maybe, but it's no different than learning to drive a car for the first time. Use expressions such as "I can and will..." "I have the power to..." "I am capable of..." and "I'm proud of myself for..."

And here are more tips from a December 2020 article in the *Wall Street Journal*, with my own thoughts added after each.

- **Take time to grieve.** We've lost so much to COVID, some of which we're not getting back. It's okay to feel bad about that; in fact, it's totally natural. Grieving what we've lost allows us to move on.

- **Reach out to loved ones.** I'd add "friends" to this tip. The more you're around people who make you feel good about yourself and remind you who you are, the better off you'll be. Similarly, the more negative influences you can avoid, the better.

- **Create a routine.** This goes to fashioning a sense of normalcy to the New Normal by forcing regimen into the mix. It helps remind you that you're still the same person you were before the pandemic, and you will either get back what you've lost or come to grips with dealing with what you still have.

- **Be nice to yourself.** It's easy to beat yourself up over the struggles that have adversely affected the people you love the most as well. But it's not your fault, and you're doing them no favors by turning yourself black and blue. Always remember that this pandemic wasn't your fault and you did everything you could to mitigate its effects.

- **Consider seeing a mental health professional.** It worked so well for me when I was treated for post-traumatic stress disorder at Home Base. We all want to believe we can get our mental health back on our own. Well, if you tear a ligament in your knee, do you perform surgery on it yourself? No! Set aside the stigma—go seek help. You'll be so much better for it.

- **Try meditation.** Or anything else that takes your mind off the mud beneath your feet, anything that helps lift you out of it. Exercise is a great prescription for this as well. If nothing else, just go out and take a walk; you'll be surprised how much better you'll feel.

- **Seek out support groups.** Misery loves company, as they say, and hearing the tales of others walking in the same mud helps you realize you're far from alone. And commiserating with others is great therapy in its own right, while helping somebody else might just be the best therapy of them all.

- **Do something new.** Taking on something fresh is like a mental vacation, a great way to steer your mind away from obsessing about where the pandemic has left you. Read a good book, a novel, or a classic that will temporarily remove you from the effects of all this stress.

- **Take a comprehensive view.** In my mind, this means considering your plight in the long-term context instead of the short. Then ask yourself what you can control that will help you emerge better on the other side of this.

- **Don't tie your self-worth to your work.** The job might be gone or much different, even lower paying, than it used to be. You may have changed employers or careers, but a career is a means to an end. So, focus on the ends you want to achieve, even if the means need to change.

FAIRNESS

Steve in Panama for Operation Just Cause in 1989

CHAPTER 5

BUD/S for Beginners

Being good is easy, what is difficult is being just.

—VICTOR HUGO

I f we've learned anything from the coronavirus, it's that life is anything but fair. To see so many people struck down while still in the
midst of full and robust lives, robbing their families of loved ones,
lends a whole new meaning to the word "injustice." Their deaths
will leave lasting scars on those they left behind. And, unlike scars
of the physical variety, these can't be concealable beneath a layer
of makeup.

There is also the economic injustice that has shaken millions
of lives and families with so many finding their incomes drastically
reduced or lost entirely. Jobs they may have loved and dedicated
themselves to gone; their dreams stripped away with them. Retirement plans and college funds thrown into precarious jeopardy.
Every basic tenet of life so long taken for granted lost. If you played
by the rules and did the right thing, went the thinking, you would
succeed, if not flourish.

Not anymore.

So many of us feel as if the rug has been pulled out from under our feet. We're left to fall with no way to brace ourselves for the coming impact. That turns every day into a grueling exercise in survival, at least in the figurative sense. In a sense, the feeling reminds me of the BUD/S training all SEALs must complete. An endless grind in which no two days are alike, yet all are the same, filled with being tested to the ultimate limit. It's almost like we're all in BUD/S now, only the challenges are mental and emotional without adding the physical element to the mix (except for those still struggling to recover from the virus).

I've already mentioned those endless lines at food banks, people lining up at midnight at a distribution center that doesn't open until nine in the morning. That is anything but fair, anything but just, for a man or woman who just a year earlier never had to wonder where their next meal was coming from. Indeed, the helplessness so many of us continue to experience today is rooted squarely in the unjust nature of the plight in which we find ourselves.

And yet I find the application of fairness, from those Ten Essential Qualities of an Underwater Demolition Man, to be another effective strategy to lift us from the mud in which we find ourselves. And showing you how is the mission statement of this chapter.

Leaving One Home and Finding Another

When I was young, my parents used to try their best to treat us equally and fairly, whether it be discipline or reward. I believe we all try to do that as parents, but somehow it gets lopsided. My older brother resented me growing up because he received the majority of the discipline. But to be fair, I was an observer. I watched what he did and if he got slapped for it, I didn't repeat his mistake. I thought it was pretty straightforward and simple.

When I left home to enter the Navy, it got a little harder to observe and predict who were the ones to model my behavior after. When I first left home there seemed to be a freedom that came with it, but there was also anxiety. Hell, I was still only a teenager when I enlisted in the Navy. I watched my Chiefs the closest and respected their "saltiness" and figured they only got that way through experience.

I did my best. While in the Fleet I tried to be the best sailor I could be so I would get my reward of getting orders to BUD/S. It wasn't hard. In order to be treated fairly in the Fleet, all you needed to do was be on time, have a haircut and shave, have your uniform squared away, and do the job you're assigned. Pretty much it in a nutshell. My Chief told me that on day one when I reported to the ship.

When I got that reward of orders and was in BUD/S, I looked to my older classmates for that role model and found a few. We were a wild bunch because we were really only students, and as far as responsibilities went it was our class, our squad, our boat crew, our roommates, and ourselves. Our job was to learn how to be Frogmen, pass our tests whether they be physical or academic, and to not give up, don't fucking quit.

My roommates and I had a secret weapon, though. We had spirit and brains. Max (who you met in chapter two) went out and bought a coffee maker and every Monday morning before our personnel and room inspection he would run into town and get a box of doughnuts. When the instructors got to our room they ignored the tiny imperfections, ate the doughnuts and drank the coffee, and passed us on the room. We never failed an inspection.

While we were in First Phase, I had a girlfriend who lived in Phoenix. I met her when I was in the Fleet and she was in San Diego visiting. I used to take a direct flight there from San Diego about every other Friday night and spend the weekend relaxing with her. What I didn't account for one weekend was the time change in the spring. You know, moving the clock forward one hour. Arizona doesn't observe it, but California does, making things a little wonky. When I got to the airport on Sunday evening for my one-hour flight back, I discovered it had already left in order to account for the time change. I was screwed! I called my squad leader and let him know I'd be on the first flight the next morning. What I should have done was rented a car and driven there, but my girlfriend's father convinced me otherwise. He feared I'd fall asleep and crash.

When I showed up late the next morning I was panicked. This was two weeks before Hell Week, and we were still getting our asses handed to us on a daily basis. I'd missed the Monday morning inspection and PT (physical conditioning). By the time I got there, my class was doing surf passage with our small boats as I stood beside the Bell waiting to have my ass chewed and most likely dropped from training. Lucky for me this was the '80s and not everything was so black and white; the Phase Master Chiefs were allowed some gray area and judgment with their discipline.

I got mine. After cranking out a ton of push-ups, I was led into the First Phase Master Chief's office and screamed at for what seemed like an hour on how fucked up I was and how I let my classmates down. My boat crew was doing surf passage one man short. I was instructed by the Master Chief that I would memorize the entire training schedule day by day, hour by hour for the next two weeks leading up to Hell Week. I thought that was easy and fair.

Now came the icing on the cake. It wasn't just my class schedule, it was for the two classes ahead of us as well! The Second Phase guys who were in Dive Phase and the Third Phase guys who were currently on San Clemente Island but coming back to the Strand and preparing to graduate. I had to memorize all three class schedules for the next two weeks. On top of that, I was given the humiliating task of having to spit-shine the Master Chief's boots for the next two weeks every day. So, on top of the daily task of training to be a Frogman, I was memorizing class schedules and shining Master Chief's boots. He gave me thirty-six hours to have the schedules memorized. Tuesday afternoon, at the end of our training day I had to be prepared to recite it all to the Master Chief.

Tuesday came. My roommates helped me memorize and drilled me in between evolutions. Max and Jimmy probably had it memorized as well from all the drilling. Running to chow, I rattled off the schedules; Max and Jimmy listened. Eating chow, Max and Jimmy grilled me. Every opportunity I had to review and memorize, I did.

That afternoon we were wrapping up our last evolution. We were wet, sandy, and exhausted standing on the grinder in formation. Our class leader reported to our proctor, Chief Tulas. In my head I was panicking and hoping that we would be cut loose and I would be let off. I didn't make eye contact with any of the cadre. Just as we were dismissed and turning to run out of the grinder, I heard the roar of Master Chief Tyson calling my name

"*Giblin!*"

Ah fuck.... My classmates quickly wished me luck as I did a running about-face and headed back into the gauntlet of the waiting instructors surrounding the Master Chief.

"Drop and start pushing them out, you shitbag!"

And so I did. Push-ups until I couldn't do any more. When I collapsed on the grinder from failing my last push-up, I was told to start cranking out flutter kicks, a brisk, alternating up-and-down movement of the legs simulating swimming with fins. All the while Master Chief was grilling me on the schedule. He had another instructor, Petty Officer Gary Jackson, looking at the schedules making sure I didn't miss anything.

And so it went for roughly the next hour. Me doing push-ups and flutter kicks, getting yelled at for being a shitbag and putting my own selfish desires before my classmates and training. At the very end I was spitting out the last day of the schedule and I had brain-lock. You know, that moment where you know you know it, but you can't remember for the life of you what it is. I was in the push-up position (plank for you yoga folks out there), and I was racking my brains trying to remember what the hell it was. Up until this point, I had nailed it. Three class schedules for two weeks, hour by hour, evolution by evolution. I was now stuck on Third Phase and their last evolution.... What the hell was it? Master Chief and Instructor Jackson were squatted down right in front of me. Master Chief waiting, calm and cool, and Instructor Jackson with a look like, "Well, shitbag, what is it?" Cue the theme song to *Jeopardy*.

"Graduation, you moron! Something you'll never do!" Master Chief screamed at me.

It shook me to my core. This salty Vietnam veteran SEAL was telling me I would never graduate, that I was destined to fail. Maybe not that day or the next but maybe during Hell Week or after.

What he was really doing was teaching me a lesson that I took with me throughout my career. He could have just dropped me from training thirty-six hours prior to this. No emotion. No yelling. Just the plain, simple fact of telling me I was done and to go report to the Chief Master at Arms, a chief appointed to carry out or supervise disciplinary and other duties at the command, in this case supervise the trainees who either quit or were dropped from training until they got orders back to the Fleet.

He gave me a second chance and to understand the gravity of what I had done, but at a small price. Push-ups and flutter kicks until I failed was nothing compared to being dropped from training. I was doing all of this in the shadow of the Bell. Just me, the Master Chief, and Instructor Jackson. My real second chance was to correct my selfish behavior, to be a better swim buddy, boat crew member, squad mate, and classmate. This was a wakeup call. I hadn't treated my Teammates fairly, but the Chiefs had been more than fair with me.

I could have "rung out." In BUD/S, if a student wants to quit, they have to ring the Bell three times, signaling they're done. You then set your green helmet on the sidewalk adjacent to the grinder, next to all the other helmets of the trainees who quit before you.

Almost a chronology of that class's "quitters." Instructor Jackson offered me that option throughout the course of the hour that I spent with them "chatting" about the schedule.

This didn't make me tough and it didn't make me a special case to the First Phase staff. All I was to them was another idiot trainee who screwed the pooch and was walking the fine line until the next guy did something to one-up me and shift the spotlight on him.

Fairness in an all-volunteer force comes in many shapes and sizes. Some have severe consequences, and some have little to no consequence.

During my last tour, before I retired, I was a Master Chief at BUD/S. I did my best to be fair whenever I dealt with a student. I did my share of yelling and handing out discipline as a Master Chief, and it was never fun. As a Command Master Chief at a Team, I was responsible for the removal of seven Tridents from enlisted SEALs who failed at meeting our standard. Those decisions weren't taken lightly, and the recommendation to the CO fell on my shoulders to give.

Fairness in life isn't cut-and-dry like the military. There isn't a code of conduct that you can reference to give you those left and right limits. Civilians are left to their own moral principles to guide them, and we see sometimes that they're way to the left or right of what we may believe to be true. The truth always lies somewhere in the middle.

Or remember the story about the cop who let me go after I'd broken that kid's car windshield? He could have treated me harshly, could have even arrested me. Instead, he treated me fairly, evaluating my actions in the context of the bigger picture.

What This Means for You

That bigger picture is what I'd like to focus on here.

This pandemic has taught us a lot about ourselves and our fellow citizens, neighbors, and friends. The virus isn't fair; it doesn't discriminate who becomes ill and who doesn't, who lives and who dies. Some are put through some incredible challenges, alone and struggling while our loved ones look on from a distance. Others are able to be at home, in quarantine, but still surrounded by the ones they love. I can't make heads or tails of it all, and I am truly sorry for those who have suffered the most. Life, in this case, isn't fair. But we still have to move on and move forward if we want to succeed. We have to.

It comes down to perspective, that bigger picture. I might be venturing a bit into the weeds here, flirting with the esoteric, but zooming out I genuinely believe that one of the best strategies to combat the unfairness that has become epidemic (no pun intended!) in its proportions is to go out of our way to treat other people fairly. Undertaken with the very real possibility in mind that they might be going through something just as bad as I am, or worse.

A Prescription for Healing

Titled "How to Be a Fair Person," the following list comes from the video *Fairness* in the ten-part DVD series *The Six Pillars of Character.* Let's explore how each of these truisms can be applied to the New Normal and how they can help us walk through the mud.

- **Treat people the way you want to be treated.** Never has a kind word meant so much and never before has it been more important to be sensitive to people's feelings. In the SEAL Teams we pride ourselves on the notion of brotherhood. Well, we are all brothers and sisters in the struggle to reclaim our lives and will have a better chance to succeed in that if we treat others who are similarly challenged with the respect and dignity everyone deserves.

- **Take turns.** In my mind, this pertains to not going it alone. Share the burden instead of taking it all on your shoulders.

Pain hurts, right? And if you want to relieve it, get to know your limitations and never be afraid or reluctant to ask for help with anything from handling the shopping chores to carpooling the kids. In the New Normal, the simplest challenges are often the most difficult to overcome.

- **Tell the truth.** This has never been more important or vital. As the saying goes, "The truth will set you free." In this case, the truth is one of the things we're left with in this muck-riddled abyss. Confronting the truth of your predicament allows you to conceive a realistic plan to escape it. This is no time to be riding unicorns.

- **Play by the rules.** So hard, given the fact that we already tried that and look where it got us? Except playing by the rules didn't get you into this mess, just as playing by the rules might be one of the things that gets you out of it. The rules are what we're left with when all else is stripped away, and the New Normal is likely to place a powerful emphasis on honesty and not being ashamed to admit your failures and foibles. We are no longer defined strictly by who we are: we are also defined by who we want to make ourselves into.

- **Think about how your actions will affect others.** Absolutely nothing is more important in making our way through this chaos than compassion and empathy. Knowing others are experiencing the same pain and hardship you are leaves all of us in the same boat. And the more we consider the feelings of other people in our behavior, the faster we'll be able to recover together.

- **Listen to people with an open mind.** You never know where a fix or solution might come from. When mired in an ongoing crisis, our tendency is often to shut others out and ignore their words. The problem with that is it smacks of self-pity. The more you listen, the more you open yourself up to the possibilities that come your way, any one of which might lift you from the mud.

- **Don't blame others for your mistakes.** In this case, we aren't here because of our mistakes, but blaming others for our plight serves nothing and no one. Nor does blaming ourselves. In the case of this pandemic, no sense lies in blaming anyone. That's indicative of looking backward instead of forward. As *The Lion King*'s wonderful Rafiki was fond of proclaiming, "It's in the past." And that's where it should stay.

- **Don't take advantage of other people:** Exploit others and you risk becoming stuck in a different kind of moral mud, one that is even more difficult to extract yourself from. One of the best strategies you can pursue when struck by the effects of this pandemic is to be able to look in the mirror every morning and know you're as good a person as you were before your feet lodged in mud and that you've never chased success at the expense of another's failures.

- **Don't play favorites.** I'm going to approach this one a bit differently by saying to make *yourself* the favorite. In other words, never stop believing in yourself because when you lose that faith and confidence you risk sinking deeper under the mud to the point where you're swallowing it and have to struggle to breathe. In this case, that's a metaphor for the struggle to live the way you want to. It may not be the same as before, but never stop believing you can be everything you were before COVID and more.

SEAMANSHIP

Deployed in Thailand on long rage patrol toting an M60 machine gun, two months after operations in Panama

CHAPTER 6

American Grit

True grit is making a decision and standing by it, doing what must be done. No moral man can have peace of mind if he leaves undone what he knows he should have done.

—JOHN WAYNE

The word "grit" means doing "a particular thing in life and choosing to give up a lot of other things in order to do it." It could also be defined as "perseverance and passion for long-term goals" or "resilience in the face of failure, but also having deep commitments that you remain loyal to over many years."

However you choose to define it, we're going to need all the grit we can muster to deal with this New Normal COVID-19 has left us. And right along with grit we need determination and resolve to get us through this. Remember that list encompassing the Ten Qualities of an Underwater Demolition Man? One of them, seamanship, is described this way: *only a man who is a competent seaman can truly command respect.* And that competence, in my mind, requires the very grit, determination, and resolve we all need now.

First and foremost, becoming a good seaman requires becoming a good man or woman. And no seaman worth his salt gives in or gives up when things get hard. He or she bears too much responsibility to their Teammates or shipmates—they are family.

Like your family.

You want to be the best man or woman you can possibly be not just for yourself but for those you care about and who care about you. We're all being tested now as we've never been tested before. Passing that test means finding the grit, determination, and resolve required to refuse to knuckle under. "When the going gets tough, the tough get going" might be a cliché, but that doesn't make it any less true. And the mission statement of this chapter is to define the kind of toughness that will make your walk through the mud less of a slog.

Pete

I gained entry into my assault team, self-described as "the Pirates," at DevGru. Shortly after I got there, two Green Teams after me, a guy named Pete showed up. He was an officer, but not your average, run-of-the-mill (if there is such an animal) SEAL officer.

He was older and a Virginia Military Institute (VMI) "Rat" and a Navy Chief's son. He grew up hard and lived a hard life. His summers in the 1960s while at a storied military academy were not spent at home relaxing but at the school doing cadet summer training. He was dedicated to his purpose. After VMI he went directly into the Marine Corps as a fresh second lieutenant. His first tour as an infantry officer took him to Vietnam in the early 1970s, serving under then Captain Oliver North. After he was finished with his commitment to the Marines, he decided he'd try his hand at construction and civilian life. It suited him, to a degree, but not as well as the military. He liked the discipline but not the rigidity of the Marines.

So, he entered the Navy, first as a Diving Salvage Officer. Not an easy route, but for Pete, life wasn't about being easy. As a person who always seemed to take the road less traveled, he decided the SEAL Teams sounded better, but by this time his age clock was about to run out for a crack at BUD/S. He was in great physical shape, no doubt about that, but he was thirty-four years old, racing toward thirty-five, which was the age limit for entry into BUD/S. He was in constant contact with his Officer Detailer at BUPERS, the Bureau of Personnel for the Navy. His Detailer was a captain, three grades above him, and Pete pestered him continuously with phone calls requesting a shot at BUD/S.

One day, while the captain was meeting with his boss, a rear admiral, he mentioned this persistent lieutenant who wanted to go to BUD/S but was too old and, given the attrition rate, probably wouldn't make it. The admiral asked if his physical scores were good and the captain said they were. Additionally, he added, his fitness reports and his rankings within his command were above his peers. So, with that, the admiral said "let him go" and made the captain a $100 bet that Pete would make it through BUD/S.

A bet might be how Pete made it to BUD/S, but his own grit and determination is how he got through, the same grit and determination that defines seamanship according to the Ten Essential Qualities of a Frogman.

Pete would graduate the Frogman school and move to the East Coast with his wife and join his new brothers at SEAL Team 8. Pete loved being a Frogman, a SEAL, and everything that went with it. Like most Frogmen, he knew he'd found his tribe, his clan, and he embraced it with full gusto.

His next step, after completing his Platoon Commander tour, would be to get an interview at DevGru and get a ticket to the dance for yet another challenge in his life with the best of the best. VMI, the ultimate school of hard knocks, wasn't enough. The Marines wasn't enough. Neither was being a Navy salvage diver. Pete wanted to be a SEAL at the tier-one level.

Pete made it through the assessment and selection of Green Team and was accepted...in his forties. Hell, I was twenty-six and thought it was tough; I couldn't imagine being "old" like Pete. He wasn't the first "old guy" to complete that training, but he certainly was a member of a very small group of tough bastards.

When he checked into our assault team he was assigned to my tactical element, Alpha, unofficially known as the Wrecking Crew. We had fun, trained hard, and prepared for combat every day. His time as our Assault Element Leader was only about a year or so when he found himself in charge of the entire assault team. He was now a Team Leader, one of only six in the entire DoD. The icing on the cake for a guy who got into BUD/S on a $100 bet because he was "old."

Now this is where life gets tough for Pete. He was an Assault Team Leader and still expected to do everything we do: dive, shoot, clear buildings, assault underway ships, jump from planes, and fast-rope from helicopters with full combat loads. He had the option of operating with whichever element he wanted within the Team, and he balanced it all very well. He knew each of us intimately, what made us tick, and he could make us do what he needed us to with just the right words.

Pete was a leader of men who were at the top of their game when it came to being a SEAL, or even SOF. His schedule was longer and harder than the life of a typical Assault Team Element Leader, which was already long. Besides his daily duties of leading and operating with the team, Pete and the Assault Team Chief had the additional duties of daily intelligence briefings as well as meeting with the operations officer and the top leadership of the command: the CO, XO, and CMC. They were also in charge of laying out the training, alert, and deployment schedules, individual evaluations, and so on. Management and leadership of a tier-one, fifty-five-man assault team was long and hard work, but Pete loved it. He'd very much found his purpose.

On one particular trip, a parachute training exercise out west, we conducted high-altitude jumps during the predawn hours and well into the day, five and sometimes six days a week. These can be exhausting days already, and then you had the additional responsibility of keeping yourself fit, getting food and some sleep to recharge the batteries, and then do it all over again. These trips were usually two weeks in duration with four to five jumps per day. Doesn't sound like a lot of jumps, but the packing of your own MT1X parachute and gear prep for each jump takes time. These were usually ten- to twelve-hour days.

Pete was jumping with my assault element on this particular day. It was what we would call a routine day, and we'd already completed our predawn combat equipment jumps and were now doing our day jumps. The routine predawn jump usually means everyone showing up at 2:00 a.m. for the gear prep and jump-master brief in order to be exiting the aircraft from twenty-five thousand feet well before the sun rises. You're getting your coffee at 7-Eleven while the drunks are still out around midnight.

Back to the routine day jump... As we were "stacked up" in the air and coming in on our final approach to land, Pete was swept up by a sudden dust devil and slammed to the ground. He must have been seventy-five to a hundred feet up. It's as though the devil himself pinpointed and hand-selected Pete from our stack. "Here you go, fucker! Try this on for size!" And *wham!* He was driven into the ground with his parachute and combat equipment.

His bone jutted out of the side of his soft leather assault boot, a spiral-compound fracture. The rest of us landed on the drop zone around him, and a group from the other assault element and our medic, realizing Pete had taken a serious hit, rushed from the parachute packing area to his aid. Pete, still running on adrenaline, struggled to get up and recover from what he thought was just a shitty landing. He was tangled in his rucksack and hampered by the weapon on his side, not realizing he had broken his leg. A guy we jokingly called Large Robert, a fellow SEAL and assault team member, with all the tact of Yosemite Sam, shouted to Pete amid the chaos, "Be still! Lay down, Pete, you're all fucked up!" I guess he meant well.

I was last in the stack and didn't get there until almost everyone else had already gathered around him. We knew he would be out for a while, but just how long, we had no clue. Devastating to Pete and to us. Our leader was down hard. As it turns out, this was the beginning of a new chapter of struggles for Pete, not what he was used to, out of the fight indefinitely because of circumstances completely out of his control.

His resilience and his grit were typical "Pete," though. Like the scene from the movie *Monty Python and the Holy Grail* where the guy who gets his limbs cut off one by one, Pete displayed the grit and fortitude of a knight still willing to put up the valiant fight while mortally wounded. As Pete attempted to heal, though, he encountered setback after setback with his leg. He had to wear a "leg halo," a metal contraption with screws around it so the bone could heal correctly. He was forced to scoot around on a wheelchair, and guys just watched as he blew his way down the passageway into Operations, where he was now assigned. He probably could have taken half days or milked the leg thing for months and just sluffed around, but that wasn't Pete. He drove himself to work, was there early, and left late. Typical Pete.

His disposition on the exterior was great. He was upbeat and positive, optimistic even about his leg and his career. This, too, was Pete.

Finally, after about a year of struggling with his leg not healing, fighting off infection and the excruciating pain, the tough decision was made to amputate just below the knee. We knew this was hard, but we didn't know just how much harder it would get.

Yes, the relief from the pain was there, but now Pete had to struggle with being an amputee in the military. Had there ever even been such a beast? In the 1990s, let alone the SEAL Teams, that answer would be a definitive *no*. Even for a guy who was now in Operations and doing it well, despite the medical issue. Hell, we all thought, why not keep him on in that sort of capacity, as an operational planner? He had the rank (now a lieutenant commander), the skill, and way more intelligence in his little finger than most of the SEAL officers who were his peers at that time.

Navy rules, though, written in black and white, stated that amputees could not jump, dive, or do all the other things that came with being an operator in the Teams. The Navy probably even had a policy on one-legged pirates.

Our chain of command had no other option but to comply. I have no idea what was happening behind the executive-level closed doors in the Coronado headquarters, or in our command for that matter, but what I do know was that Pete wasn't taking anything short of, "Yes, you can stay."

He started reaching out to his VMI buddies, looking for options, in search of a recourse. How could he find a way to stay in, still serve? He would get his answer with another bet, of sorts.

A VMI classmate, now a lieutenant colonel in the Marines and working in the Commandant of the Marine Corps Office at the Pentagon, had heard of Pete's plight through the VMI alumni network. The Navy was forcing him out, giving him his pink slip. His friend knew Pete and knew he had so much more to give.

This lieutenant colonel explained Pete's situation to the commandant, whom he had direct access to. The icing on the cake for the Marine general was the fact that Pete was a SEAL officer at a tier-one unit and before all that had been a Marine infantry officer. As the story goes, the commandant reviewed the options and walked into the Navy's Chief of Naval Operations' (CNO) office. Paraphrasing what he said, "You have a SEAL officer who's being forced out just because he's missing his leg below the knee. He was a Marine officer before that, and I'd like to take him back into the

Corps." The CNO took that information and called the head SEAL officer at the time, a rear admiral in Coronado, to inquire about how to respond.

But the CNO knew the Marines would make good on their word and didn't want to be shown up. The determined Pete would have to prove himself by means of the Navy Physical Readiness Test (PRT) and pass within SEAL standards, better than Navy good. Then a medical waiver would have to be granted with regard to a prosthetic and doing what SEALs do so he could continue serving.

As it turns out, he was introduced to an amazing doctor who fitted him with custom prosthetics for walking, running, and swimming. While all of this was happening, Pete worked down at Fort Bragg, at JSOC, in the Operations Department.

I had to do a temporary tour down there as an enlisted liaison for our command—three months that none of us looked forward to. The commanding general wanted a senior enlisted from both tier-one units who knew the inner workings of their respective commands, how they operated, and could be relied on to be that conduit between the various operations departments. The assault team Troop Chiefs all rotated down there after their Alert Cycle and worked in the J3, Operations. This was my turn in the barrel. I went to Fort Bragg to work at JSOC, in Operations with Pete. Pete was the current ops officer in the J3, the office next door to where I was; he was the J33. His job was to stay abreast of everything JSOC related regarding day-to-day operations and to brief both the Army Special Forces colonel who was the head of Operations and the JSOC commander, at that time an SF major general.

While I was there, I had the pleasure of having nightly dinners with Pete, forcing him to leave before 8:00 p.m. and to get a healthy meal since his wife and kids were still at the beach in Virginia. I also had the privilege of first taking Pete to the wind tunnel and then on his first free-fall jump since he was initially cleared to stay in. In the wind tunnel we got him back to that familiar feeling of "falling," but now we had to figure out how to manipulate and function with the prosthetic limb. Once he was comfortable after several sessions in the tunnel, we transitioned to the actual free-falling from the aircraft. The scary part was making sure he had a smooth landing with the new limb. Opening shock could jar that puppy loose and really put a damper on a landing.

His first landing was anything but graceful. I landed first and ensured I was there to watch him come in. Since I was using a much smaller parachute, I was able to get down quicker and take it off before he landed. This was all preplanned with Pete. When he landed, he hit and tumbled like he was jumping a static-line chute. I shit a brick. He gathered himself up, turned and looked at me, and grinned. I never saw a happier guy. He was headed back with a full head of steam! This was one of several milestones he needed to complete, both physically and mentally, in order to get back to the world he loved so much, and no awkward parachute landing was going to stop him.

After getting fitted with the other prosthetics for running and swimming, he trained for the next big milestone: his PRT. Pete passed with flying colors using both. The swimming leg, as he called it, could lock the foot at the ankle with the toes pointing downward and the fin would strap on like any other. There was time in between each event where he could switch legs and drive on. He practiced the transition like a triathlete trains for the transition between the swim and running events in a race. This was the guy who made it through BUD/S on a bet because he was "too old," and now he would become our first SEAL with a prosthetic leg to remain on active duty.

When Pete was the CO of SEAL Team 4, at the same time my wife was there as his Admin Chief, the command would do their daily physical training sessions on the grinder and then run, go to the obstacle course, or swim—sometimes all three. And Pete would tell the guys, "Don't let the chicks beat you!" What he really should have been saying was, "Don't let the one-legged old man beat you," which apparently happened more often than not.

Grit and determination are what I first think of whenever I see a picture of Pete. Those were second only to his unparalleled leadership, which I'm very proud to say I've been a recipient of, as was my wife. In other words, he was the perfect seaman with a never-quit attitude who never faced an enemy he felt he couldn't beat.

He would serve as the Special Boat Unit 20 CO, operations officer at DevGru, then as SEAL Team 4 CO and Naval Special Warfare Group 2 commodore with plenty of in-between tours. Pete wasn't done, though.

He and I were both assigned to work overseas in Iraq for an officer who at the time was a one-star real admiral (lower half). We both knew the admiral well and had good history with the man.

Pete, as a captain, would be his chief of staff and I was in the J3, Operations Senior Enlisted Advisor. Pete's leadership to our staff there in Iraq was invaluable during a very critical turn in the history of that war and the mission of the command we were assigned to, setting up the Iraqi SOF and their Intelligence Center, among other things.

While Pete and I were there, the admiral received word that he would be the next WARCOM commander, officer in charge of all SEALs and SWCCs, and was promoted to his next rank, rear admiral (upper half). He still had another six or seven months to go in the current tour he was in, and he wanted Pete there with him to finish out the tour successfully. He extended Pete, but in return gave him his dream job.

Very shortly after the admiral stepped into the WARCOM commander role, he gave Pete the best assignment of all: commanding officer of Naval Special Warfare Development Group. It was during his time as CO of DevGru that the boys got Osama bin Laden. I saw Pete at the compound three days after that, and you couldn't wipe the grin from his face, just like after that first jump with the prosthetic leg. He couldn't have been prouder of the command and the Naval Special Warfare community. Hell, who wouldn't? Enemy Number One since he'd orchestrated 9/11 was EKIA, or enemy killed in action.

And Pete got to play a major role in that because his grit and determination wouldn't let him walk away, on one leg or two. Because he was the perfect seaman.

What This Means for You

Let's go back to the definition of seamanship, to the kind of resolve that commands respect, like Pete's. Another thing that's part of seamanship, especially when it comes to the Teams, is working toward a common purpose and relying on the strength you've developed to get you there. Sure, I'm talking about physical strength, but I'm also talking about intellectual and emotional strength.

You hear someone referred to as "strong," and the first thing that comes to mind is physical. Even more, though, the strength we need to deal with the New Normal falls into the other two categories as well, as it did for Pete. You can't gut your way through BUD/S relying only on physical strength, any more than you can through what our world has become without the intellectual and emotional strength that makes you as gritty, determined, and resilient as Pete was in his unrelenting desire to be every bit the man with one leg as he had been with two.

Think of Pete losing a limb as a metaphor for all you've lost, how your life has changed and been redefined, since COVID entered our lives. Pete not only fought his way back, he made himself better, good enough to climb the command ladder to virtually the very top, defined by perseverance and grit. Pete didn't let such a setback stop him in his tracks, and neither should you.

A Prescription for Healing

But how best to accomplish this? The list below all sounds so very simple, but the idea is you have to practice it every day. Make it your own personal code to live by. Let's call it "Pete's Code."

- **Core values.** These aren't just words on a page; they represent a standard that we expect our government and society to live by on a day by day, hour by hour, minute by minute basis. Having core values makes decision making easier, and it makes going to bed at night a more satisfying experience knowing that you did the right thing.

- **Be courageous.** Courage is not the absence of fear; it's feeling the fear and doing it anyway. Don't second-guess a goal that is worthwhile. Don't believe in fearing failure. Believe in yourself, the bigger picture, and the rewards to come if you're moving in the right direction.

- **Be proactive.** Don't wait for things to go wrong or pile up before taking action. Face adversity before it shows up at the doorstep. Being proactive leads to a life that looks easy to the rest of the world, but all it takes is implementing forethought and putting you ahead of the curve.

- **Take ownership.** Blame no one but yourself for your mistakes. What matters most is solving the problem and taking matters into your own hands. So never oppose responsibility; you have it, act accordingly. Embrace it!

- **Know it's always long-term.** Forethought, every decision we make, is about the long-term benefit.

- **Foster relationships.** The people we share our time with gives us the ultimate fulfillment. Give more than you receive and make sure that every person you come in contact with leaves better than when you first met them.

- **Be of service.** Serving the community and the world around us is the ultimate contribution we can make to the world. Even when we are "on the clock," we are there to be of service. Make decisions based on what is best for our fellow human, not what's best for ourselves.

- **Make learning a lifestyle.** Learning is repeated, habitual, not just a one-time affair. Become open minded in your view of the world and constantly seek information that both challenges and builds upon what you already know. Science shows that the only way to get better is to learn something new every single day. If you learn something new every day to get 1 percent better, how much better will you be in a year?

- **Be hopeful.** Believe that we are always around the corner from a better life. No matter what your current circumstances look like, have the grit to see it through.

- **Communicate well.** Listen with open ears and an open mind. Nothing is more vital for maintaining healthy relationships, a thriving career, and persevering through day-to-day challenges.

- **Find simplicity over complexity.** Don't overthink life. The only easy day was yesterday.

- **Do more than just make your bed.** Be willing to make the beds of others too. And don't fret if the bed you're sleeping in now is smaller than your old one. Someday you'll not only be back where you belong, but your bed might even be bigger than it ever was or you ever imagined it could be.

SINCERITY

Steve presented with an award by the Joint Special Operations Command commander for his participation on an operation in Bosnia

CHAPTER 7

Defining Character

*Reputation is what you are perceived to be
and character is what you really are.*

—JOHN WOODEN

Character is what defines most if not all of us in life. Some seek to better their character and others just go along and allow it to develop and be what it is. Neither is a bad approach. But your character is what will ultimately define you at work, in your social life, and privately. If you've got a personality like a bent trash can, then you would be well advised to seek ways to improve yourself or settle and continue to go through life with few friends, and those you do have will most likely be cut of the same cloth. Life can be hard like that, but you don't have to live that way.

In my mind, it all comes down to sincerity, one of the key elements of character. Bad times tend to bring out the worst in people. Scammers and schemers crawl out of the woodwork with any number of opportunities and offers that seem too good to be true—because they are. I won't bore you with a list of the biggest ones that have plagued us during the pandemic, but the lot of them has left us appreciating sincerity all the more. I can tolerate a lot in people, but if I can't trust someone, if I know I can't take them at their word, the relationship stops there. I've also been on the other side of that as well, let some people down. I've lived and learned.

"As we express our gratitude," President John F. Kennedy once said, "we must never forget that the highest appreciation is not to utter words, but to live by them."

Sincerity is one of the touchstones of the SEAL community. I can cite plenty of times when I've been disappointed by this or that by the men within my command, but I can't name a single one where I didn't feel any of them weren't being sincere, especially when the shit hit the fan. There's no place for liars, fakers, or phonies in the SEAL Teams.

In fact, there's no place for liars, fakers, or phonies anywhere.

"Sincerity in society," W. Somerset Maugham once wrote, "is like an iron girder in a house of cards." The point is this: we only continue to function as social beings by playing by the accepted rules of the game. So, the mission statement of this chapter is to highlight how we need to be genuine and sincere now more than ever, that our character is a crucial element in how we navigate the New Normal.

Perception Management and Reputation

Perception management is a term used widely by the US military, at least in the Special Operations world that I came from. Perception is defined as the "process by which individuals select, organize, and interpret the input from their senses to give meaning and order to the world around them." Components of perception include the perceiver, target of perception, and the situation. People can use perception management as a way to positively enhance their personal character reputation. A person's ability to manage perceptions about themselves is what sets great leaders apart. What people, your followers, appraise as your effectiveness and ability as a leader becomes their perception, which then becomes reality and ultimately defines your character. If you are sincere, you have nothing to worry about. But if you've built your reputation along any other lines, you've constructed a house of cards that is destined to collapse.

Perception management can be hard work, but it can help us all grow as leaders and individuals, so once applied effectively, it becomes easier from then on. The decision-making process in relation to the future is an element of business that has a great effect on any organization's success. If the organization is overly risk averse, this leads to underperformance and missed opportunities. If an organization takes too many risks, it's likely that it will face a large number of losses. Ultimately, if this amount of risk-taking leads to the perception of the organization exceeding the boundaries of logic and fact, it will most likely fail based on its poor perception management, its reputation.

The reputation of that team of reckless pirates I was a part of led to us being less likely to be selected as the option, or force, of choice for a variety of specific missions. Most generals and admirals despised our rogue character and overlooked our capability until 9/11 when the sincerity of our commitment made them look beyond their perceptions of us. But those perceptions still trailed us like the chains dragged by Jacob Marley, Scrooge's deceased business partner in the Dickens classic *A Christmas Carol*.

I learned this the hard way as a leader. After being dismissed as Team Chief of my assault team, after all was said and done, I realized I didn't do anything to help myself or the assault team I was leading as their senior enlisted. I wasn't being as sincere as I should have been with them or with myself. I guess I just threw up my arms and got pissed off and took what happened personally when in fact it was the Team and the command's reputation that was really at stake. I failed to recognize the bigger picture.

Right, wrong, or indifferent, the reason and purpose of my Team Leader and me being relieved wasn't because we were bad leaders. It was the perception that had been created from the actions of the men we led. The "pirate culture" had gone too far.

When people think of the SEAL Teams, they usually think of the guys that got bin Laden and other dramatic events. Sure, that works. The DevGru guys; you know, SEAL Team "Them." But it really only captures a fragment of the true essence of an organization that's been out there for many decades, doing some very hard work. From the beaches of Kwajalein and Normandy to Korea, Vietnam, Grenada, Beirut, Panama, the Balkans, and the Middle East, SEALs have faced and fought adversity.

Yes, we have our boneheads who've done some really stupid shit, and it just seems to keep getting worse before it gets better. Those are the 10 percent that lack sincerity and whose purpose as a SEAL somehow gets muddled—only 10 percent, yet they overshadow the other 90 percent out there doing really good stuff. I mean really *great* stuff, rescuing hostages in the middle of the Somali desert kind of great stuff.

When we went through training, we never thought to ourselves, "Yeah, I want to be a 10 percenter, that friggin' guy who takes up 90 percent of my leadership's time dealing with my bullshit." Some have fallen into that category. Others, like me, have dipped their toes in it, and some managed to avoid the predilection altogether. A lot of times a person's character, and I mean true character, doesn't come out until sometime after training is finished, and I don't mean just the bad ones. I mean all the people. The stoic professional, the wild one, the uptight guy, the troublemaker, on and on. The thing that the 10 percenters all have in common is a lack of sincerity. Something about these individuals keeps you from embracing them all the way as Teammates. It's like they have an ulterior motive or something, the kind of people you like less the more you get to know them because you don't fully trust them. They make being a "dick" a full-time job.

When my BUD/S class was in Third Phase comprised of land warfare, demolitions, and weapons training, we were out on San Clemente Island finishing up the end of the twenty-seven-week program. At this point in BUD/S, a guy would finish this portion and then go on to Army Airborne School at Fort Benning, then on to their Team, wherever that may be. In total at that time, it was close to eight months of getting your ass handed to you day in and day out.

Exactly what we all signed up for.

Back to "The Island"

We were there on San Clemente for an extra week because then governor of Nebraska, Vietnam-era SEAL, and Medal of Honor recipient Robert Kerrey was scheduled to speak at our graduation but couldn't make it until a week later than our original graduation date. The training cadre were getting short on ideas of what to have us do for more training. We'd already done our five-mile ocean swim. We'd blown up all of our demo and shot all of our ammo, and then some. We ran and did our PT every day. Talk about cleaning, the camp was probably the cleanest it had ever been.

So, we ended up doing more patrol and recon exercises. Patrolling the island and sneaking and peaking around Wilson Cove and sketching and taking notes. On one particular night, while sitting in wait for a high-value target to appear, I got sleepy. I dozed for only a few seconds, but I got caught by one of the training cadre, Instructor Dave Piana. When we returned to camp after completing the exercise and debriefing, cleaning our gear, and so on, I was called into the Master Chief's hut. I recalled this feeling from First Phase—not good, to say the least. In there was the Third Phase officer in charge, Master Chief Huey, and Instructor Piana.

If I could say I got reamed, that would be an understatement; matter of fact, that would have been a blessing. I can't even put into words, still, as to what I got in there. The most royal ass-chewing of all time? It sure felt like that, and it made me feel like the biggest shitbag of all shitbag students who ever graced the Island. When I left the hut, my stomach hurt, my mind was spinning, and I knew I was done.

The next morning while we were all hanging around waiting for the word on what we would do that day, I was called once again to the Master Chief's hut. Inside was the OIC and Master Chief Huey and nobody else. The OIC told me I was done and that Master Chief would take me to the airfield and I would fly back to North Island on the regularly scheduled rotator flight.

"Go pack your seabag, Giblin, and meet Master Chief out front."

That was it. Twenty-seven weeks of training, Hell Week, pool comp, log PT, boats-on-heads...all of it gone because I was a shitbag and dozed off while on a recon.

I understood, but it was killing me I couldn't look any of my classmates in the eye. My class leader and lead petty officer asked what was going on, and all I could choke out was that I'd been shit-canned and was packing up to fly out. The class was stunned. I was packing up when four buddies came in and gave me their condolences. Funny thing, three of them were at my retirement party twenty-six years later.

What we didn't know, none of us, was that there weren't any flights out on Sundays. We were so busy training we didn't pay any attention to the day or anything else that went on outside of our bubble.

But the show went on. Master Chief met me out front and we walked to his jeep like a hangman leading the condemned to the gallows. I threw my seabag into the back and climbed into the passenger seat and we drove off.

We arrived at the airfield and Master Chief told me to take my seabag and go wait in the departure lounge, if that's what you call an aluminum-sided Vietnam-era Quonset hut. Nonetheless, I did what I was told. Nobody else was inside. It was quiet, and I was alone with my thoughts. I didn't feel sorry for myself. What I was really good at was beating myself up. About fifteen minutes later Master Chief walked in and angrily told me there weren't any flights that day and we needed to go back to the camp.

This was worse than the departure from camp! Now I had to go face these guys, my classmates, or should I say former classmates. Oh God. The hurt in my guts got worse. When the Master Chief and I climbed back into the jeep, rather than starting up the engine he started to speak instead. He told me he knew there weren't any flights, and all this was to teach me a lesson: never fall asleep in the field. "Your teammates' lives depend on you and yours on them," he said. He also said that my personal reputation in the class was good and my performance in BUD/S to this point was good, so I was given a second chance. I guess he didn't talk with Master Chief Tyson about my little "faux pas" in First Phase.

He then explained to me that the phase OIC was addressing the class as he and I had been sitting there at the airfield, and he was explaining the same thing to them. He wasn't getting sappy with me; he remained stoic because quite honestly, he didn't know me from the next guy. I was just some kid who was going through training, just like the other 150 that year who passed through his island and the hundreds more the years prior.

This still made facing my classmates a challenge, but now I could look them in the eye. As we rolled into camp the class was busy doing field day, cleaning up the barracks, chow hall, and class-room. I slipped into the barracks with my seabag and proceeded to unpack what I needed and put my stuff away. As I was doing this, a good buddy of mine, KT, came up and told me what they knew from the phase OIC and that he was personally relieved I wasn't shit-canned. That made me feel good. As the morning went on other classmates told me the same thing, almost to the man.

This all happened during our final days on the Island. I tried to remain low profile, but because of the recon-napping incident, it was tough. I did a lot of push-ups, pull-ups, and dips as a penance, and when it came time to do our "flights" up Frog Hill, I paid the man with extra rounds.

Flights up Frog Hill were basically us running as hard as we could two hundred yards up a steep hill with a shipping pallet, wood or metal depending on the severity of the points you collected, or a large metal turnbuckle across your shoulders. Get to the top, knock out fifty push-ups, and run back down without killing yourself. Before each flight an instructor read off your name, what this flight was for, and what type of equipment you will be flying— wood pallet, metal pallet, or turnbuckle, which were all associated with a certain type of Navy aircraft. All of the instructors were there and enjoyed watching the class perform this ritual. Maybe this was the genesis of CrossFit? Who knows?

At this point we were just a day or two away from packing up, cleaning camp, and getting back to the Silver Strand and prepping for graduation and then off to Army Airborne School. We were relieved, especially me. Sometimes, you don't realize how important something is to you until you're on the verge of losing it.

The day before we were to head back to the Silver Strand, we were packing up and closing the camp in preparation for the next class's arrival. Something had happened that triggered one of our classmates, Dave W., to get the attention of "Pinky," a Senior Chief and a West Coast SEAL Team Vietnam veteran. He seemed to us to really know his shit when it came to teaching and supervising demolitions and land-warfare tactics training like ambushes and patrolling.

Dave was a "legacy" student, meaning his father was a Team Guy, coincidentally a teammate of Pinky's back in the day. Unfortunately for Dave, he was mediocre at just about everything we did but managed to scrape by. In timed four-mile runs, he was our dead-last guy. Ocean swims, he and his swim buddy were near the rear. Obstacle course, Dave was last. He just wasn't a dynamic individual. Most of us had no idea his dad was a Team Guy.

Usually when an instructor strode up to a student in the manner that Pinky did, people stopped what they were doing and observed because you knew the shit was going to hit the fan. This incident was no different. Pinky started laying into Dave about his lackluster performance throughout BUD/S and then he went into a diatribe that not even the other instructors saw coming. It all finished with, "You're a piece of shit...just like your old man!"

Holy shit! You could have heard a grenade pin drop on the entire island. Dave was crushed. We, the students, were dumbfounded. And the other instructors were aghast at what just happened. Nobody knew why. Maybe Pinky saw something nobody else did. Maybe something else was gnawing at him. Master Chief Huey pulled the Senior Chief into his quarters and that was all we saw.

We did our best to rally around Dave in a quiet manner and attempt to lift his spirits. Graduation was in less than two weeks and we'd be gone. The remaining day and a half at the island was uneventful, with the exception of the "Pinky-Dave" incident. My napping issue seemed to be overshadowed by that one, not that I was relieved, but it did take some heat off. I still felt like shit, though.

Graduation

Adding a little salt to the wound, the governor cancelled his engagement to speak and we ended up with a Navy captain from the amphibious fleet as our guest speaker. We graduated and moved on, all heading to jump school with the exception of the three guys who went to SEAL Team 2. They were going directly into their Team's SEAL Tactical Training (STT), which was kicking off later that month. They would get jump qualified after that.

At jump school Dave seemed to rebound and became his usual self. The PT there seemed to be more his speed, and there weren't any timed events or crushing workouts, which was all well and good with Dave and the rest of us. We made the best of Airborne training and messed with everyone else as often as we could.

On the morning of our fifth jump, our graduation jump and week three of Airborne training, the Marine liaison officer approached and informed all of us Navy and BUD/S graduates that five SEAL operators had died that morning while inserting in heavy seas for Operation Urgent Fury. He didn't have any more details than that, but it resonated with us because of what we were getting into; this business of Special Operations was some serious shit.

By the end of that week, we were all headed to either our Team or home on leave. I was going home on leave, or to my girlfriend's home anyway. You remember—that gal in Phoenix. I was relieved that my basic training for being a SEAL was over, and I was stoked to be headed into the new life I'd been training for.

When I got to Little Creek two weeks later, I started running into my former classmates who were already there. The guys who were at SDV with me were doing FNG work, meaning they were all dispatched to the various Team departments to assist in the daily life of supporting the platoons. I wasn't any different—I would be going to the Diving Department, better known as Sub Ops, with Max and Carrick. The few lucky new guys that checked in after BUD/S who got to go to Air Ops would usually get their next five jumps sooner than the rest of us, shedding their Army lead jump wings for a shiny gold set of Navy wings and when they got their Trident the set would be complete.

I wasn't so lucky. I'd have to wait another nine months or so before myself and a few others got the gold wings. We got our Tridents pinned on us at quarters, and we still had lead Army wings. I didn't wear mine; I guess to a large extent I was still a kid, too full of myself to leave room for growth. I had a problem with sincerity, but not because I'd ever lie, either blatantly or by omission. I was insincere in the sense that I wasn't being honest with myself and that was holding me back and affecting my reputation in the process. I handled all the physical challenges just fine, but something about my wild-child attitude kept some of the SEAL Team leadership from fully believing in me. In the SEALs, that belief has to be 100 percent. No room for any margin of error. Looking back, I think maybe the Chiefs thought I needed more time, more seasoning. Because maturity eliminates the need to lie to yourself. You look in the mirror and the person you really are looks back, not the person you're pretending to be.

In other words, the first person you need to be sincere with is yourself. If you can't be sincere with yourself, don't expect to be able to be sincere with anyone else. The one thing everyone I've known who gets stuck in the figurative mud and can't get out has in common is this very tendency. And, yes, I've witnessed it in plenty of SEALs as well; we're human, too, after all.

One guy who was sincere as it gets was Art Fusco. He was twenty-three years old and everybody loved him. I first met him in my BUD/S class, but he was rolled back after Hell Week into the next class because of an injury. He taught me how to fix my wetsuit top in BUD/S. How a guy from New Hampshire knew this I had no idea, but he was good.

We were all still pretty tight and one morning when he and I showed up to our Team area parking lot at the same time, he asked if I could help him carry in his deployment bags. Naturally I did and all the while we were shooting the shit. He was always happy and that day especially because he was headed out on his first deployment with the Teams to Central and South America, which at the time was SEAL Team 4's area of responsibility, or AOR, as well as the Mediterranean. He was put into the platoon early and deploying only one year after graduating BUD/S, meaning he went to STT, then jumped into the platoon's workups midstream because they were down a man.

Only two months later we got the bad news. Art and his platoon were trying to clear a logjam in a river that had isolated some local villages in Honduras. After setting explosive charges, he and a Special Boat Team operator apparently failed to move far enough away in their Zodiac craft and were caught in the blast. Both were killed. Whoa. Our first classmate fatality. It hit us hard. Art was the guy you loved to like. His reputation at the Team was awesome as well, the guy everyone liked to be around. That infectious work ethic. The drive. His grit.

And, yes, his sincerity.

What This Means for You

There are several ways to define sincerity, but I tend to go with simply "no bullshit." There's no time or place for bullshit when you're training, prepping, or deploying for missions, not when somebody else's bullshit can leave your life hanging in the balance. Trust has to be absolute, nothing to weaken or dissipate it. You can't compromise in that respect, not when you're behind the lines in the dark of night surrounded by the enemy. Insincerity makes you a lousy Teammate, which means there's no place for you in the Teams.

If only I knew then what I am writing about now. I guess that's what comes with age sometimes, a bit of wisdom. Why does this chapter seem important enough for me to include it here? Just look at what's happening around us, the insanity, or at least perceived insanity. If we keep running at breakneck speed in every direction, we won't be able to discern what the hell is really going on around us enough to slow the hell down, take a deep breath, and make the changes we need to. Positive ones. Whether it's politics, work, or our personal lives and daily living, what you do out there matters, and people are watching and forming opinions of you.

Getting ahead of that bad reputation has to start with you, the individual. If there is any doubt about your own personal character and what is reflected outward, start with some steps to help guide you.

Don't force yourself into damage control every day. Stop and think before you act impulsively.

"The secret of success," the French dramatist Jean Giraudoux wrote, "is sincerity."

Plan to use it as your calling card, now more than ever.

A Prescription for Healing

Obviously, a conflagration of crises like the ones that have plagued us for what seems like forever can gravely threaten a person's reputation. That's because, even if you're trained for a crisis, bad times tend to bring out the worst in too many people, turning them into poor likenesses of themselves. How, then, when faced with a crisis, or even multiple crises, can you "keep your head about you while others are losing theirs," as Rudyard Kipling wrote in his famous poem *If*?

- **Sort through your motivations.** Honestly understand the motivations that created the dilemma in the first place and were driving you toward the decision you made.

- **Ask others for advice.** Seek counsel with a peer or mentor you respect and who will keep your conversation confidential. As you seek an answer to a difficult question, try to gather as much information about the situation and what your options might be. You want to make as informed a decision as possible. One part of this "research" phase is asking for feedback from friends, family, and mentors.

- **Study the question.** What is causing the situation? Are you in the middle of it and, if so, how can you extricate yourself?

- **"Why do I always get caught up in drama?"** If this is the situation or dilemma, maybe you're part of the problem— you didn't cause it, but your actions are only making things worse. Maybe someone from the outside looking in can provide that perspective. I oftentimes failed at this, asking someone their perspective, and my ego was often to blame because I wasn't being sincere with myself.

- **Think about what you've learned.** Before reaching that final conclusion on what you need to do, bounce it off that person you sought advice from. Someone you trust, someone who'll tell it like it is even if it's something you don't want to hear. You need people like that in your life. They keep you real, keep you grounded.

- **Let it settle.** My mom used to say, "Let it simmer awhile and you'll know." Sage advice for sure. Don't come to your first conclusion and then act impulsively. Sometimes letting an idea "simmer" will allow it to refine or even come to a full and more complete understanding. A good example would be writing that email or text message in anger and shooting it off before letting it simmer. You might find that you will end up changing or deleting it all together after some thought and time.

- **Move forward with confidence.** Even if you feel absolutely sure of your decision, you will still question yourself about it sometimes. That's completely normal. But you can't retreat from your decision and go back to straddling the fence and be constantly asking "what if?" Like one of my Platoon Chiefs used to say, "If you spend too much time thinking about a thing, you'll never get it done." Meaning, fence-sitters end up with one piece of themselves on one side and another piece on the other; they fail to progress and miss out on the benefits that walking fully down either path would have brought them. Instead, when you have times of doubt about the decision that was made, simply reflect upon the decision-making process you already went through to get where you are. If the conditions upon which you made your decision have not radically changed, feel assured that you made the right choice and move forward. That's what's so powerful about this process—rather than just making a big decision willy-nilly by default, you can always look back and know you did all you could do to come to the best decision possible and continue to embrace that choice and live with confidence. That's being sincere with yourself.

EXAMPLE

Steve while serving during OEF in Africa in 2003

CHAPTER 8

Women Who Serve

I love to see a young girl go out and grab the world by the
lapels. Life's a bitch. You've got to go out and kick ass.

—MAYA ANGELOU

Not just a legendary female warrior but also a Roman Catholic
saint, Joan of Arc was but a girl when visions of the Archangel Michael drove her to approach the military of France's King
Charles VII and offer to assist in his efforts to expel the occupying
English in the later days of the Hundred Years' War. Though initially mocked by these men and soldiers, Joan was taken seriously
once her influence ended the Siege of Orléans in nine days.

By age seventeen, she played a key role in commanding France's
army, and her forte in the military seemed to be for strategy over
slaying. The French owed much to Joan, and yet it was the Burgundians, Frenchmen loyal to England, that led to her demise.
She was captured in 1430 and, despite several escape attempts and
rescue efforts, Joan was put on trial by the English for heresy and
cross-dressing. Her visions were now derided and her armor called
an atrocity. She was convicted, sentenced to death, and burned
alive at the stake.

Even after her death, her strategies are said to have influenced the French battle model. More than twenty-five years later, the Catholic Church revisited Joan's trial for heresy, overturning the charges against her in a case of too little too late. It would be more than 460 years before Pope Benedict XV declared Joan a saint.

Digressing a bit, the mission statement of this chapter is to illustrate the example set for all of us by the Joan of Arcs of today—women who serve in Special Operations in particular, and the military in general—and what we can learn from them.

Today's Joan of Arcs

Women in the SOF community are nothing new, even as quasi-operators. With today's operational tempo it's a wonder that this concept has taken so long to emerge as normal or really take traction at all. The problem is that every flag and general officer in SOF is committed to upholding the sacred training standards of their respective organizations, which should never change in their minds, as far as women serving in combat goes.

And that's what makes the women who choose to buck the system and prove themselves the kind of example we should all aspire to. To that point, I believe the people, men and women, best equipped to deal with the New Normal are those who refuse to take life at face value. Instead of accepting what's served up to them, they grab the spoon and dish it out themselves.

"I have always been driven to buck the system," Sam Walton, founder of Walmart, once said, "to innovate, to take things beyond where they've been."

Taking things beyond where they have been requires thinking out of the box, and thinking out of box is what you need to do in order to emerge on the other side of the mud better and stronger than you were when you found yourself slogging through it. The notion of warriors who happen to be women is an apt metaphor for that, given all they have to overcome in their journey to become special operators. Hell, the odds are against any male serving in Special Operations, never mind a woman.

Are there women out there who could pass the training without sacrificing or compromising the standards? Sure. As of this writing there has been at least one woman who has passed Green Beret training and several who have passed Ranger School. Naval Special Warfare has had women pass certain training gates, only to drop on request later in the process. A dream deferred, but not destroyed. The time of women as operators in SOF will come, setting a shining example for all of us to follow. And, as Albert Schweitzer once said, "A good example has twice the value of good advice."

Not Always Smooth Sailing

My personal experiences with women in SOF started in 1987 as I was checking out of my first Team and headed "across the street" to my new command and Green Team. I was standing in the Medical Department waiting to get my records and check out of the command. The Medical Department at the time was right in the center of the East Coast Teams' compound, so to gain entry you had to go through one of the three Teams' quarterdecks. Standing beside me, waiting to check in, was a young female corpsman, a medic. The first on the East Coast to be assigned to a Naval Special Warfare command. What I didn't know was there were many more to come.

In my own ignorance, I was chuckling inside. She was cute, and I knew there were going to be issues. Fraternization. Sexual harassment. You name it, it was coming her way. As I was driving away from Little Creek, I was thinking, "Damn, I'm glad I won't be around for that shitstorm to hit."

Within the hour I was checking into my new command. The big boys. The varsity squad. I was an FNG all over again, and I was hoping to make it among the fabled Green Team. The place where most of my peers wanted to go, though few made it through the tough selection process.

My first stop was the Administration Department inside the main building. They handed me a check-in sheet and told me each one of the places to report to. Medical. Disbursing. Supply. Training. Security. Intel. All located within the confines of the compound fence line.

I first went to the Training Department and was greeted by one of the members of the cadre. Not a warm welcome, but nonetheless I was told where my cage would be, who I would be sharing it with, and who was available to help me finish checking in. My cage mate was a fellow Green Team guy whom I knew from Little Creek. He came from SEAL Team 4, and we were only a couple of BUD/S classes apart from each other.

George showed me where our cage would be and how things were set up, basically half and half. I looked at all the shelf space and asked if this would be filled up. He laughed and said we get duplicate sets of gear and we'd use it all. It was packed! We literally had to get changed outside of the ten-by-ten-foot cage. At the Team I just came from, I had two kit bags, diving and land warfare, and a double-door metal locker that held my uniforms and essential daily things such as PT cloths and shower kit.

We went to lunch and while we ate, he filled me in on what to expect over the course of the next couple of weeks as we waited for the rest of the guys to check in. We were getting SEALs from all over the community, to include NSW units from overseas, BUD/S instructors, and so on. When all was said and done, we would have about thirty or so guys in our Green Team.

We still had about three weeks before training started, so I had time to get used to the command and get a rhythm going. While we waited for training to start, we would get farmed out to the assault teams and the snipers to do everything from "pulling butts" on the rifle range to "pulling chutes" for water jumps and being a role player bad guy for hostage rescue scenarios. We didn't care. We were stoked that we were just there and given the opportunity to try out.

When we returned from lunch, George showed me where Supply was and told me to make sure I got everything on the Green Team supply list. I figured this would take an hour or so and then I could sort through it all in the cage area. Took me two hours, as things turned out.

When I walked into the Supply building, I was greeted by Michelle. Holy crap, a female! I guess she saw the look on my face and she gave me attitude right out of the gates. I apologized and asked her how long she had been there, and she replied about two weeks. We chatted while she and I went around and filled my bags, checking everything off the list. It was like a shopping trip to L.L.Bean, Bass Pro Shop, and REI. I got civilian gear bags, body armor, and at least seven pairs of boots! Leather pistol belts, nylon pistol belts, and traditional military LBE web belts. Three sets of magazine pouches for the CAR-15, MP5, and Beretta 92F in addition to speed loaders, pouches, and a drop-leg holster for the S&W 686 and 92F. Several knives of various types. A Leatherman multitool, which I still have.

It was a crazy first day and not just because of the gear. In a scant few hours, I'd met two women assigned to NSW—women in SOF! There would be many more after that, and we just got used to them as they got used to us. It wasn't all roses and unicorns, though, and there was a steep learning curve for the guys.

We baby boomers of the US military had essentially been raised in a misogynistic culture. I was surrounded by salty old Frogmen who were of the same ilk, and I knew there would be issues and tough adjustment periods, even for me. Women were objectified and were not assigned to warships or other units within the Navy and military in general at that time. Getting an assignment for them that actually fit their idea of joining the military was rare, but it all started to change in the 1980s.

Michelle was a special case, though. Her assignment to that command at the time was significant for so many reasons. The place was special in its own right, and when the issue down in Panama rolled around only a year later, she would really fit right in. She was bilingual. Fluent in Spanish, she would prove to be an integral part of Operation Just Cause; not just the mission, but the whole period leading up to it.

She was pulled from her duties in Supply, assigned to a new job within the command, a special "cell," and trained by the best guys in our command in the art of everything she needed to know for her new role, a female SOF enabler and later, an operator. She was schooled in the latest and greatest tactics, techniques, and procedures for intelligence gathering and tradecraft. She was taught to shoot, move, and communicate in a way that would save her and the guys she was teamed up with.

An operational cell was established specifically for this geographic region. They would travel in and out of the Canal Zone and operate in conjunction with our sister organization and other national agencies. The beauty of these types of units back then was that they could be as creative as they needed to be in order to get the mission done. That remains the protocol today, as long as their actions fall within the legal boundaries, Title 10, of doing so.

This was stuff ripped from the pages of the OSS manuals of World War II, and Michelle was right in the thick of it. I didn't know what to think about it all, while some of the other guys thought it was crazy. Kevin, my soon-to-be shooting partner in our assault team crew, was wise beyond his years, and he explained to me how this sort of stuff worked, and he helped me see through my own ignorance and lack of emotional intelligence. I worked with Michelle once, one-on-one as a jumpmaster and Military Free Fall (MFF) coach, to quickly help improve her newly acquired skills so she could, if required, infiltrate into an area with the rest of her team. All options needed to be on the table.

This was 1988–1989, and women in SOF were still more of an intrusion, a heresy to the culture of manly men. After Operation Just Cause, the cell was disestablished due to various reasons and, I dare say, lack of vision. Michelle was reassigned back to Supply.

So here was this sharp, intelligent, and now well-trained SOF female who was plucked from a support role within our tier-one organization to do some really great work, and she's told she needs to resume her duties as a "box kicker" again. I understand the CO, CMC, and his immediate executive staff had their reasons for doing things. But it just seemed almost comically odd that this would happen despite the best efforts of several senior and seasoned operators within the command who argued that the cell should remain, Michelle included, and the mission of that cell be developed and refined just as our sister tier-one unit had done.

Michelle had a decision to make. Mel, one of the plank owners of our command as well as one of that cell's senior operators and architects, advocated for her to do a lateral transfer to our sister tier-one unit at Fort Bragg. After all, they'd kept their "Panama cell" operational and even expanded it. She fit right in. I didn't run into her again until the mid-1990s in Bosnia, where she had continued to do great work. She retired from the Army as a senior NCO and, from what I hear, is living a great life as a former SOF operator.

Senior Chief Shannon Kent also broke into the "Manly Men Club," so to speak. She mastered signals and human intelligence and throughout five combat deployments persuaded unwitting or even witting people to give her information. Her intelligence work eventually led to the death or capture of some of America's most wanted foreign adversaries. She was tragically killed in action in Syria doing the work she was trained to do, directly taking part in SOF operations just like her OSS sisters had done and just like

Michelle. Thank you, Shannon, for your selfless sacrifice. Rest in peace, sister.

Our command would start a cell again about ten years later and just in time for the war in Afghanistan. From what I understand, there are now plenty of "Michelles" serving as special operators and doing great things, just like Shannon who died a hero.

Legacy

Deborah Sampson, a participant in the American Revolutionary War, was the first recorded female soldier in US history. Her appearance—tall, broad, strong, and not delicately feminine—contributed to her success at pretending to be a man. This is what she had to do, wanted to do, in the name of freedom and liberty. She served in several units, one being light infantry, considered to be elite at the time. She served from 1782 to 1783 and was wounded in a skirmish outside of Tarrytown, New York, taking two musket balls to the thigh and a gash to her forehead. A doctor treated her head wound, but she left the hospital before he could attend to her leg out of fear her gender would be discovered. She removed one of the musket balls herself with a penknife and sewing needle, but the other was too deep for her to reach. She carried it in her leg for the rest of her life, and that leg never fully healed.

After the war she married, had children, and eventually, after much effort, received a military retirement. Deborah Sampson died of yellow fever at the age of sixty-six on April 29, 1827, and was buried at Rock Ridge Cemetery in Sharon, Massachusetts.

Women such as Sampson and Harriet Tubman deserve to be a bigger part of our nation's great history, right up there with Paul Revere and Sam Adams. Harriet Tubman was born into slavery in Maryland in the 1820s. As you could imagine, her early life was filled with serious hardship, but that was the norm for people of color in that day and age. Physical violence was a part of daily life for Tubman and her family. The violence she suffered caused permanent physical injuries. Tubman later recounted a particular day when she was lashed five times before breakfast. She carried the scars for the rest of her life.

As is well known about Tubman, she escaped slavery and became a "conductor" within the Underground Railroad, helping other Blacks escape the bondages of slavery. She was fiercely independent and brave, to the point where she carried a bounty on her head because of her courageous actions.

In 1858 Tubman was introduced to the abolitionist John Brown, who advocated the use of violence to disrupt and destroy the institution of slavery. Tubman shared Brown's goals and at least tolerated his extreme methods. Tubman claimed to have had a prophetic vision of Brown before they met. When he began recruiting supporters to raid the US arsenal at Harpers Ferry, he turned to "General Tubman" for help. After his subsequent execution, she praised him as a martyr.

Tubman remained active during the Civil War. Working for the Union Army as a cook and nurse, she quickly became an armed scout and spy based on her reputation and skills in the field from prior years. She was the first woman to lead an armed expedition in the war, guiding the Combahee River Raid that liberated more than seven hundred slaves in South Carolina.

The example of Harriet Tubman is just another that makes the case for why women can and should serve in SOF in operational roles, not just support. Just like the men who serve, they are fully capable of providing enormous combat effectiveness and intelligence to the battlefield. And what a great example pioneers like Harriet Tubman, Deborah Sampson, and so many others have already set for all of us.

Where We Go from Here

If a woman is good enough to be deployed into any combat zone for service on the front lines alongside SOF operators, she deserves an opportunity to earn a permanent operational position within any SOF unit. Standards shouldn't change to accommodate them, or any candidate for that matter, but something needs to be figured out to draw greater numbers into the fold. One possibility would be to extend SOCOM's own women-only SOF selection and training course.

We now have SOF units that conduct special missions in just about every corner of the world, many under the radar, and women are a part of that but maybe not as much as they need to be. Women often have a sense, an intuition, that men don't. It's an internal mechanism to help keep them safe from real danger, a warning light if you will. Men usually don't have that, and that's okay, because we need men who will be the first test pilot or that first guy to jump out of an airplane with some silk and strings. We need the women to be the sanity check sometimes, that yin to the yang, complimentary to the men.

Women are critical to the success of SOF, whether they are an enabler or an operator. Like any organization, civilian or military, the recruitment and retention of these highly qualified and intellectual individuals must be brought to the forefront. Just as important is the reality that everyone, including civilians, have a role in the recruitment and retention of women in Special Operations, the military, and our national security.

I worked with a handful of career officers who I respected very much; we were friends, and I believe the feeling was always mutual. What they taught me was this: as long as you aspire and strive to do more, learn more, and improve your circumstance, you will always be successful. I was routinely given assignments that were matched with mid-grade or above officers both stateside and overseas. I helped run exercises and operations alike, standing shoulder to shoulder with officers from the other services and our SOF brethren.

My wife learned this as well, but not until she served in the SOF community, which is a shame because that tells me the regular Navy and military at large had not changed all that much, or at least not as much as it should have up to this point. In our civilian careers we were both senior and working with contemporaries within and from outside the SOF organization. We ran into situations where individuals discovered that not only were we retired enlisted, but we didn't have college degrees. While I will acknowledge that a degree most certainly would have been helpful, I'll also say it doesn't replace institutional knowledge, skill, and just plain hard work.

Just before we retired, my wife was given accolades by senior civilians as well as flag and general officers at SOCOM headquarters, along with our own senior chain of command at Naval Special Warfare, for her intellect. They also praised her ability to see and understand the process for projecting future requirements within our community and setting the fiscal budget for the years forward. Not an easy task by any stretch, even for those who have a degree.

SOCOM adopted some of her methods for its own models and complimented her work and made it known that it should be the standard to follow, in spite of some others' efforts to claim it as their own. She did this all without a college degree but instead she watched, listened, and learned, earning her way up the ranks. We've come a long way, but we still have a long, long way to go.

"Changing a culture is never without headache or heartache," wrote Captain Micah Ables for the Modern War Institute in February 2019. "Racial integration of the Army was not easy, either—it had more than its fair share of stutters and missteps, from social isolation to all-black units to segregated facilities. But flawed standards and imperfect implementation are not good reasons to scrap worthy policies. We should not penalize a capable and competent minority of women because the majority may not be qualified to serve in combat arms units; instead, let's fix the real problem so that *all* of our combat forces adhere to a higher standard."

At the time, Captain Ables was deployed with the 1st Cavalry Division as commander of one of the Army's first of only four mixed-gender mechanized infantry companies.

What This Means for You

There is no better encapsulation of the qualities it's going to take to survive the New Normal than those that women in the military exhibit. They are underdogs right from the start, entering a system that is quite clearly rigged against them. They are also perceived, rightfully in some cases, to be physically unable to handle some of the rigors of training and deployment. They come in with their backs against the wall, and women like my wife spend much of their careers trying to create separation.

Well, all our backs have been against the wall for longer than we care to remember. So, let's explore the approaches that work for women who serve and see how they apply to walking in the mud.

A Prescription for Healing

- **Stick with it.** Perseverance may be an overused cliché, but it applies perfectly here. If you want to succeed in the military as a woman, you can't quit. And you can't quit in the face of the residue left by our common experiences of the past two years either. You may want to throw up your hands at times, the frustration that's been stabbing at you gaining the upper hand, and that's okay. Just lower them again and get back to the task at hand.

- **Do your job.** That's the very definition of focusing on what you can control and, when walking in mud, there may not be a lot that fits that description. Women who serve beat back stereotypes by being very good at what they do. You can beat back the New Normal that the pandemic has left behind by being very good at *everything* you do, in the workplace and beyond.

- **Don't feel sorry for yourself.** We're all victims in this so the pity card doesn't work any more than it works for women in the military. Whether right or wrong, women are held to a higher standard and not given the benefit of the doubt that men are more prone to receive. So, you know what? Hold yourself to that higher standard and stand tall as you walk through the mud. The higher esteem in which you hold yourself, the higher esteem others will hold you in.

- **Make your voice heard.** Women play an integral role in the military today, serving in virtually every capacity available. In times long past, some women would disguise themselves as men in order to fight. Those of you reading this book, men and women, need to disguise yourselves as nothing more than the person you want and need to become in order to deal with the realities imposed upon us by the New Normal. Making your voice heard isn't so much about standing out as standing up under the weight of a crisis trying to buckle you at the knees.

In full dress uniform as a SEALS Master Chief in 2005

CHAPTER 9

Warrior Spouses

Setting an example is not the main means of influencing
another, it is the only means.

—ALBERT EINSTEIN

"It takes an exceptional woman to love a warrior clan, especially a clan whose war will never cease."

I can't for the life of me remember where I heard that quote, but it might well have come from a widow of a SEAL Team operator reflecting on her life as a survivor. She wasn't overly concerned when he first deployed with the Teams. Special Operations operators are the kind of people you expect will always make it home.

But as time went on, she felt an "underlying dread" that grew and grew.

"I think I just got better at hiding it," she says. "There is so much about military life nobody will tell you, and soon I would learn just how much goes unsaid."

When she and her husband spoke on the phone, she ended every call by asking him to be careful. His frequent answer? "Everything is fine. We've all got each other's six."

After his tragic death, she returned to her hometown, moving in with her parents. She struggled with her moods.

She went back to church, thinking that might help. God is love, she heard at church. She struggled with that.

"How can God love anyone and do what he did to my husband and the other men they've killed?"

Friends tried to console her. They told her, "You're really strong. God knows you could handle this." She tired of that fast.

"I'm not strong! My husband's gone. I have no kids. Who's going to want to date a widow?"

It turns out she found companionship with a wonderful man. He's kind, attentive, and makes her laugh. They now live a happy life and have children. She says her husband was instrumental in her healing, as was her decision to seek counseling for her grief.

A key moment came when a counselor suggested she might be angry at her deceased husband. She resisted that, but then realized as much as she loved him, there was truth to it.

"I was angry," she said, "because I realized something I should have known. Being a SEAL is your first love."

With that acknowledgment came healing. That's just who he was, and she was okay with that. She accepted it.

So the mission statement of this chapter is to learn from the sterling example set by these warrior spouses who are forgotten warriors in their own right.

The Forgotten Warriors

It's quietly recognized that the spouses and children of veterans are the forgotten warriors of all the wars. For them the war never ended; often it just came home to their doorstep. The example they set for selflessness is second to none. Their capacity for sacrifice is off the charts. Their mates are serving a cause bigger than themselves, and warrior spouses know in their hearts they're serving the same cause. They understand in the great scheme of things how small they are in comparison to that bigger picture.

I see much the same thing with the New Normal, but not limited by gender. The picture is just as big, but we're looking at it through a different lens. A different war has come home, and we are all still fighting it. Recognizing that our family members are going to struggle—in school, at work, in life in general—is the first step in acknowledging that these times are like no other we've ever faced and must be treated as such. Like warrior spouses, we must learn to accept and adapt while not giving up or in. It's a question of attitude, of mindset, and if we all adopt the attitude and approach aligned with warrior spouses, the mud we're walking in will start to harden and the other side won't seem nearly as far away.

Think about how our warrior spouses often share their lives with veterans afflicted with PTSD, the devastating psychological problem that plagues at least twenty out of every hundred veterans. They suffer from vivid and sometimes violent flashbacks, chronic depression, emotional numbing, and withdrawal just to name a few. Some of these people abuse their spouses and children. Some turn to drugs and alcohol. Some even attempt or commit suicide. And all of their suffering can destroy the lives of their families as well. Call it the "ripple effect."

As we covered in chapter one, PTSD symptoms include intrusive memories, avoidance, negative changes in thinking and mood, and changes in physical and emotional reactions. The one thing they have in common is the degree to which they affect the sufferer's loved ones, especially his or her spouse. PTSD sufferers bring the memories of what they saw, felt, and experienced home with them. And those experiences spread as fast as COVID itself, infecting their loved ones by association.

Add to that anxiety the thought of it all ending with retirement. What happens next? How will I survive financially? What on earth will I do for a second act that compares to what I love doing? His or her family becomes that veteran's only true support system, replacing the whole of the military that has dropped them back into society often lacking the tools to survive there as they had done on the battlefield. It's a different skill set entirely, and great pressure is brought to bear on our warrior spouses because the burden of reacclimatization falls on them, replacing an entire military and nation that previously had their back.

The pressure isn't the same as serving, but sometimes it can be even greater.

I deployed overseas about one-third of my twenty-eight years in the Navy and SEAL Teams. That's nine-plus years deployed. Nine-plus years pre-deployment or on alert training as well, and nine-plus years of specialized training. For an operator who does their twenty, that's six and a half years of each cycle. Each training cycle replicates combat. Multiple repetitions per day, per week, and so on.

I'll be the first to admit that 99 percent of those deployments for me were not the hard-hitting combat that our operators are seeing today, but the training workups prior to those deployments were not any less. The point is, the preparation for the deployment can be just as dangerous, if not more, than the deployment itself. You're still away from your family. And I don't know what's worse: the stress of that or the stress of trying to figure out what comes next when there are no more deployments to come.

This is what tears at us inside. And, oftentimes, it's left to our warrior spouses to put us back together.

You'll recall from chapter one how I discussed my own experiences with post-traumatic stress disorder, how I'd reached the breaking point. When I got home from that visit with my father, my wife could tell something was wrong.

"Are you okay?" she asked me.

"No," I told her, "I don't think I am."

I'd already had one marriage dissolve, my first wife having not been the right fit for a man she had to share with the Teams and the country. But my second wife was the perfect fit, and I couldn't bear losing her. My warrior spouse, then, was all the motivation I needed to try to get right again, to seek the help I needed. If she could beat the odds by becoming a Navy Chief, I could get better. She proved a shining example for me, and I wasn't about to let her down.

My father was a policeman and career law enforcement. My mother resented him and the fraternity of brothers he was a part of. She didn't understand his commitment to his chosen profession, and they fought constantly. I'm sure she worried as well. She drank to relieve her stress, her pain of being left home to raise the three of us kids. She left her job as a secretary and took up waitressing in bars. The pay was better, as were the tips. But that also meant constantly being around alcohol and falling into that social setting, compounding the issues at home before and after the divorce that in retrospect, I suppose, was inevitable.

Warrior spouses face a different challenge in that the deployment of their husbands (or, eventually, wives) lasts for a year at a time instead of a day. It's one thing for my mother to say goodbye to my father at breakfast and welcome him home at dinner. It's quite another to kiss your husband goodbye at the base, knowing you won't see him for as much as a year and sometimes not even knowing where he actually is. The warrior comes home after all that time and wants to pick things up where they left off, like my father upon returning home after twelve hours instead of twelve months. And the warrior spouse has no choice but to make that so in a courageous, selfless fashion.

The experience of my first marriage left me determined to never repeat it. My second wife, Barbara, made me a better person, and I'm not sure there's a greater gift any man could receive.

What This Means for You

Setting an example by its nature means making those around you better, something these times are crying out for. What's the point in surviving or thriving alone unless you fashion yourself to be Robert Neville from the classic Richard Matheson book *I Am Legend* in which he has every reason to suspect he might be the last man on Earth.

Warrior spouses are the ultimate givers and set a shining example for selflessness, serving a greater cause even though they never enlisted. Well, we never signed up for what we're facing now either. No one I know volunteered to be walking in the mud in which we find ourselves stuck. But taking the attitude of warrior spouses is one of the surest ways to reach the other side unscathed.

A Prescription for Healing

- **Manage expectations.** Warrior spouses understand the realities associated with their mates returning from deployment. They know it's not like a child coming home from camp or a young adult from college. We all have to face the realities thrust upon us by the New Normal. Lowering expectations is cause for celebration when they're exceeded in any capacity. Sometimes difficult times require setting your sights lower, not because you're not ambitious so much as you're being realistic.

- **Be a shoulder to cry on.** When you find yourself without the support system you need, the best solution is to become one yourself. There is no better way to deal with your own problems than to help someone else with theirs. Warrior spouses know this better than anyone, and at times they have to redirect their own priorities in favor of the husband's or wife's. That's an example all of us should learn from.

- **Do the right thing.** President Barack Obama defined "quiet heroes" this way: "They're not famous. Their names are not in the newspapers, but each and every day they work hard. They aren't seeking the limelight. All they try to do is just do the right thing." That's what we all need to be, following the model of warrior spouses because nothing is a better recipe for keeping things in perspective.

- **See the bigger picture.** "See the bigger picture of yours and refuse the passport size creature that people think you are! Your nature is large; go for it. Feel free to wake up and print your bigger picture!" Israelmore Ayivor wrote that in his book *Dream Big! See Your Bigger Picture!* The bigger picture means looking at this in the long term instead of the short. Focusing forward to when the trail of mud you're sloshing through ends, instead of looking back to see where it started.

- **Look outward.** Holocaust survivor Elie Wiesel once said, "Just as despair can come to one only from other human beings, hope, too, can be given to one only by other human beings." This is easier said than done when your feet are stuck in the mud, but that doesn't detract from the credo's potential impact. In my mind, it comes down to celebrating small victories, not just large ones. Learning to find great joy in the simplest thing. You can't afford the new car you need, so get the old one detailed. And if you're not in a position right now to make yourself happy, focus your efforts on making someone else happy. Call it joy by association.

LOYALTY

Master Chief Steve Giblin serving in Iraq, OIF, in 2008

CHAPTER 10

Circling the Wagons

Loyalty to the family must be merged into loyalty
to the community, loyalty to the community into loyalty to
the nation, and loyalty to the nation into loyalty to mankind.
The citizen of the future must be a citizen of the world.

—THOMAS COCHRANE

Being loyal to family, spouses, friends, workmates, leadership, and your country. Sometimes it doesn't always come easy, but that loyalty will be paid back in spades with deep relationships, promotions, and a better place whether it be your personal life, your work life, or your life as a citizen in this country.

But loyalty has another implied or implicit meaning as well. It means sticking with someone through thick and thin. Being loyal to someone can be equated with believing in them. And this is a time for circling the wagons and keeping the people you were close to before COVID-19 even closer now.

It goes without saying that you want to be the kind of person who others can rely on, the kind of person they are loyal to in turn. And it's not just loyalty to a person. This is also a time when the company you work for, the civic organization you champion, the church, synagogue, or mosque you belong to, needs your loyalty more than ever. Remember, it's a two-way street in that you have to believe that your loyalty will be returned in kind at a time when we all need that most. "Loyalty," according to the famed advice columnist Ann Landers, "settles for less than perfect and makes allowances for human weaknesses."

In other words, loyalty is about tolerance and not being harsh or judgmental. It's about believing in someone enough to look past their flaws and recognize their strengths. And the mission statement of this chapter is to illustrate the importance of loyalty in successfully negotiating the New Normal.

Shit Happens

Nobody's perfect. We screw up, we make mistakes, have heartbreaks, go through hard times, but you need to know that this is life. We don't get to write the rules; we only have to follow them.

At my second Team, where I spent over a third of my career, we had a pretty cool plaque and to get one was an honor. It meant you were a respected member of the Team or a closely regarded friend of the Team. We always voted on who would be "allowed" or "privileged" to get one, such as when someone left the Team.

Usually outgoing commanding officers always got one in respect for their leadership of a frontline command. The plaque was designed before I got there, and the men of the Team all had input in its design and the words on it. It was meant to be a lasting tribute to the Team and those with connections to it. On the plaque was a skull and crossbones flag, a pirate flag, being held by a pirate from the 1700s and opposite an operator in his kit. On the flag, it read "Shit Happens."

I thought it was great. I was twenty-five when I entered that Team after a tough six-month selection process. I "bought in" to the ideal of that Team and its culture 100 percent. I was all in.

146

At that time, we had plenty of combat veterans of Vietnam, Grenada, and some Central American incursions. Some, but not all, were "plank owners," original members of that command when it was stood up. The CO at the time was a Vietnam combat vet, as were the previous COs and our Command Master Chiefs. The command was peppered with combat veterans, but as they retired or transferred it had to be backfilled by us new guys, SEALs from other Teams.

The Interview

To be a member of this exclusive and very selective command, potential candidates interviewed in front of a board of current team members led by a senior SEAL officer, and then it was determined if that guy was a go or no-go to get orders to the assessment and selection process. That process required six months of learning the basic standard operating procedures of the command, the Tactics, Techniques, and Procedures (TTPs).

The assessment and selection process was physically demanding and kept the operator busy with constant training in the basic skills required to be at that command. Of the twenty-seven or so additional weeks we were in this process, we were gone twenty of them. When we were home, we were still working, training, and learning, so there wasn't much rest.

We were essentially indoctrinated into that command's culture and work ethic. Holidays were ignored, weekends were for travel, and personal lives were on hold. Guys who came from the West Coast usually came out alone. One guy in my group lived out of his van inside the compound during the entirety of that process. Just like in BUD/S, guys were injured and some were de-selected by the cadre for a variety of reasons, but we didn't have anyone Drop on Request, or quit like in BUD/S. We were, after all, SEALs who had already gone through the same basic selection course, BUD/S, and had all served at a Team at least for one tour of four years.

The Draft

After assessment and selection training, you were drafted into one of three assault teams (as a side note, there are now four). The Team Leader and Team Chief of each assault team sat in a room and took turns selecting from a roster of men who had just completed the rigorous selection process. They had access to their training folders as well as input from the operators in the assault team and training cadre.

A lot of the information on each man was based on their performance over the last six months, but also from input of current assault team members who knew these guys from their previous SEAL Teams. The input from those operators had to be qualified based on their personal and operational experience with the man before coming to the command.

For the guys who were selected, sometimes it was personality based, or maybe they had specific skill sets from their previous SEAL Team that could be put to good use. On the other hand, you couldn't just say "he's a shitbag" and that was it. You had to qualify that statement with why he was a shitbag. If nobody wanted him, he could be literally let go, given new orders to either his old command or a new command. I guess that's when a guy could say "shit happens."

It's one thing to be a good operator, but another when your reputation as an individual follows you; your behavior, your personal attributes as an individual, are just as important as slinging lead and kicking doors. Assault team operators could be given orders to leave the command at any time. I knew this from the onset. You had to earn your keep every day. This was a situation where your success is never owned, it's rented. And the rent was due every day.

Back in the mid–1980s, one operator was given orders to another command because he ate the CO's sandwich out of the refrigerator. No shit. The command at the time was so small that the break room was shared by everyone. There was a couple of refrigerators, some microwaves, and that's where everyone put their food for the day or night. The guy was hungry, but he hadn't brought enough food, so he decided he would grab that tasty-looking sandwich he spied in the fridge. About halfway through that tasty morsel the CO walked in to grab his lunch and go back to his office, the very sandwich this guy was chowing on. The proverbial shit hit the fan. Next thing that operator knew he was getting new orders to another SEAL Team. Gone, just like that. Shit happens. All because he didn't give a shit, or at least enough of one.

When you enter into a subculture of something as deeply imbedded as the SEAL Teams, you buy in really hard. Such an assignment requires a 100 percent buy-in, 100 percent of your loyalty. No ifs, ands, or buts. Within the assault team I was assigned to, we rallied around the skull and crossbones flag and arm patch. Some, but not all, bought in heavily to the "Shit Happens" motto of the Team. Like other unofficial mottos of Special Operations units, not all are correct and can offend many. There isn't a disclaimer on the back of the plaque saying that the culture may offend someone.

We had a Teammate die in a parachuting accident in the '90s. Carl was a great guy and a strong member of the Team. Both of his parents were deceased, and it was unanimously decided that his sister would receive the coveted plaque in addition to a large flower arrangement. In a flash of brilliance by someone in the Team, it was decided that something had to be done about the motto on the plaque. "Shit Happens" had to be removed. So, someone took a mini-grinder to it and carefully removed the words and painted the spot black.

In the mid and late '80s, the COs of the command as well as the parent command, led by a Special Forces major general at the time, despised the skull and bones, or as we referred to them, "the Bones." We were, at that time, the only assault team to have a patch and a mascot of sorts. These are what are now referred to as Moral Patches. Typically, the only units to have patches like that were aviation squadrons, and this was something new to the Special Operations community.

What it meant to the leadership was far different than what it meant to us. To them it was a hypocrisy. To us, the shooters, it personified us. What we didn't really understand was that it was interpreted as misguided loyalty, that we were more loyal to the Bones than we were to our nation, command, and the mission.

The Team was misguided, to a degree. We were the post–Operation Urgent Fury crew, mostly, and in the past, before my time there, they had blown some major exercises and rehearsals for real-world missions. As a result, they were losing the confidence of the commander and the commanding general due to this perceived inability to execute sensitive and difficult missions. That kind of minutia aside, in 1985 the Team was on the tarmac at Naval Base Sigonella in Sicily squaring off with the Italian police and military police while the *Achille Lauro* hijackers were holed up inside the Egyptair jetliner. This after the 737 had been refused permission to land in Tunisia, home of the Palestinian Liberation Organization with asylum for the hijackers in the offing. President Reagan, eager to avoid a repeat of the botched Iranian hostage rescue mission, had ordered the hijackers be seized, leading to a standoff between US and the Italian authorities after SEALs surrounded the plane once it touched down. Ultimately, a diplomatic solution was reached without a single shot being fired.

On the surface, the government and military's faith in the team seemed undeterred. Beneath it, though, the Team Leader and the Team Chief were eventually fired for cause, not because of the standoff but because of lack of confidence, and they were reassigned elsewhere. The other two assault teams were doing fine, but the Pirates were blowing it for the rest. It was a very rocky road for the command and the assault team for several years, and it took longer than that to regain the confidence of the upper echelons. I didn't know this, or maybe I did but failed to believe how our assault team alone could impact such major impressions and decisions. Well, it did.

We were loyal to each other and the Team. What needed to happen, though, was this: we had to really start giving a shit about more than just us. We had to show more deference to the command and the overall mission. Deference isn't a synonym for loyalty so much as a part of being loyal.

In 1989 we deployed to Panama for Operation Just Cause. We were led by a great cadre of leaders, and all three assault teams and our augmented operators executed our missions very well. Sure, there were some screwups, and we tragically lost four SEALs from SEAL Team 4 as well as some SOF and non-SOF from other units. This happens in combat and war. This is what we signed up for, that risk of not coming home, that blank check. But that doesn't make it any less acceptable or tragic.

When all was said and done and we were back home for two weeks, we were in the Team Room having some beers at the end of the workday, rallied around the Bones, talking about everything that happened in Panama and elsewhere the past year, the successes and the losses.

One of the older guys, referencing the tragedy at Paitilla Airfield, said, "Well, shit happens!" That left a sting in my heart and gut. I knew one of the guys who was killed. I lost every shred of respect for the guy who said it at that time, right there. I think I grew up a little that day.

In my mind's eye, he was now a shitbag, a real first-class loser, who had disrespected and displayed disloyalty to a fallen Teammate. He never failed to disappoint as time went on, and I distanced myself as far as I could from him going forward. I could serve alongside him, but he'd never get my loyalty because he hadn't earned it. He was one of the training cadre that put me through Green Team and now he was back at the assault team, but not for long, maybe a year, two at best. I was really disappointed in him and those that chose to listen to him and fall into that toxic pool that he was a part of.

I actually looked into transferring and stopped short of getting orders. My Chief at the time, Foster (a.k.a. "Firk"), explained some things to me about life in that command and how sometimes guys aren't always a perfect fit or fall from grace for one reason or another. We also talked about who to follow, what to believe, and that the nation and mission were always first, never the Bones, and how misguided loyalty could get you into serious trouble.

I stayed around the command for another ten years and made my way through the ranks and leadership positions. I eventually filled Firk's shoes and then later became the Assault Team Chief. I don't believe I ever measured up to Firk's standards, or even Mike P's or Jay's, but I certainly tried. I did know that rent was due every day, always.

Falling from Grace

Being the Assault Team Chief wasn't easy. You were expected to lead the Team along with your Team Leader according to the CO's and CMC's direction. As in any high-performing command or civilian company, the structure is top down, not bottom up.

Somehow, I fell short on being able to hold my place toward the end of my second year. I was unceremoniously shown the door thanks to two operators who failed to give a shit and screwed up overseas. Ultimately, though, I was the senior enlisted for our Team, and their failures became mine. I owned the failures 100 percent. Ownership of the bad, as well as the good, is another component of loyalty.

The CO and CMC came to the conclusion that it was a lack of leadership within the assault team at the top, so my Team Leader and I were removed, fired, and reassigned within the greater SEAL Teams. Roger went out west to Coronado and I stayed local, going to Little Creek to help man the newly formed Training Detachment, Assault Cell. Sometimes this is how "Shit Happens." I got my Team plaque that says so.

You cannot just give a shit only *sometimes*. It's got to be every day, 24/7, caring about every single thing you do. Half-assing things will only lead to more problems, and you will only have yourself to blame. When the chips are on the table and you have to ante up and make the tough decisions, you can't hesitate to make the tough call. And if I'd made a few more tough calls, I might have kept my position. Not doing so was my decision, so I had to own it. And taking ownership is another big part of loyalty to a cause greater than yourself.

Lessons Learned

My new position at Little Creek, with the new SEAL Team Training Detachment (TRADET), was part of a greater reorganization conceived by our leadership at headquarters in Coronado. It also happened to fall just before 9/11 when our world changed radically.

I took my personal and professional lessons learned and applied them to my new role as a member of the TRADET cadre. A good friend of mine and exemplary leader within the SEAL Teams, whom you met in chapter six, once said, "You have five minutes to feel sorry for yourself or kick yourself in the ass. Then you have to put it behind you and move on." Thanks, Pete. It took me longer than five minutes, but I eventually moved on.

When I was promoted to Master Chief a year or so later and reassigned to a Team as the Command Master Chief, I took those lessons with me, every single one of them. I think it was hard for others to understand why I stood where I did on issues and my leadership principles, but they were mine to wrestle with and figure out. I was more callous now and didn't tolerate anyone's bullshit anymore. My circle of trust was much smaller.

The lessons learned from my previous leadership experience in the assault team and the ultimate failure helped reshape my new outlook. How I dealt with people and subordinates and my recommendations to my CO were more hard-line. Discipline was the rule—and not just discipline in the form of punishment, but also the discipline of leading a group of people and living up to the commander's vision. Because I had found I needed to be loyal to that vision, even if it didn't precisely mirror my own.

I found that same discipline to be true when I transitioned into civilian life. I didn't fully transition—I still worked for the government—but in that new role we still had to live up to the commander's expectations and vision.

My first job out of retirement from active duty was at our newly established survival and code of conduct course, SERE training (for Survival, Evasion, Resistance, and Escape). We were in charge of teaching the soon-to-be SEALs and SWCCs how to survive in enemy territory, handle themselves in captivity and escape situations, as well as live up to the United States military's code of conduct. There were thirty-five of us trainers, and I found myself shortly after signing on in charge of all the civilian experts who were running the training.

Yes, I worked for someone—we all do. Even CEOs answer to someone. Their board, their customers, and even our government in some cases.

But now this was a new and strange landscape for me. I wasn't a Master Chief any longer but still needed to wear the hat. My officer in charge gave me the direction to follow, my orders, and we were to execute those orders. Thankfully, Steve was easy to work for and with, and when the hard discussions took place, we each knew our roles. Believing in each other created a loyalty between us.

The group of people I was in charge of were all prior and retired military, so they also knew what needed to be done. Some needed to be let go. Some needed to be warned, put on notice that I wouldn't tolerate bad behavior, insubordination, or subversion. Corrections were made and we trained our students. After a year we were rewarded with a very positive rating from the governing authority for SERE, the Joint Personal Recovery Agency (JPRA). I also moved on to a more permanent role in government work as a DoD civilian, but my loyalties were no less guarded or clear.

That new role involved making multimillion-dollar decisions and following direction and guidance from our admiral and his immediate subordinate leaders, my bosses. For some reason I couldn't find the job that was easy and laid back. That was the challenge, I suppose, and a debt I felt I owed to my community where I had spent so much time. My rent was still due every day, and I wanted to make shit happen, but in the best way possible. That's part and parcel, above all else, of being loyal to a cause greater than yourself. Such loyalty allows you to look past the setbacks and idiosyncrasies, your eyes forever on the bigger picture because something you're loyal to is worth it.

What This Means for You

That bigger picture has never been more important, providing us with perspective in this precarious, and often perilous, time. In times like these our circles tend to shrink, and those we remain loyal to, and who are loyal to us, take on added importance. They were the ones who were there for us before all this, remained by our side during it, and will be there in the aftermath.

But that same bigger picture requires that you grow with it. Every post, every base, every operation, every mission I was ever on came with its own set of rules. And we all have to face the fact that we are facing a new set of rules now. That means your old way of thinking, your old mindset, may no longer apply. This doesn't at all mean moving on from those you're closest to and who have shown the most loyalty to you. It means being open to exploring new roads and the new people you'll meet along the way. Exploring the bigger picture means just that, and it certainly beats walking in mud.

A Prescription for Healing

- **Know your tribe.** "Tribal" is a word used a lot these days in derogatory fashion to describe the current state of the country. In challenging times, though, surrounding yourself with those who know and understand you the best, as well as the reverse, is never a bad idea. One of the consequences of the pandemic was the extent to which our isolation kept us from venturing out beyond our circle, out of our comfort zone, even as that zone was often shrinking. Seeking solace and security from those to whom you're loyal and who are loyal to you is an effective strategy to help guide you through the muck.

- **Explore beyond the comfort zone.** Eleanor Roosevelt once said, "Do one thing every day that scares you." An ambitious and potent bit of advice, except in a time where there's plenty to scare us already. In point of fact, it could be argued that we left our comfort zone behind when we started walking in mud, thanks to this pandemic. "As you move outside of your comfort zone, what was once the unknown and frightening becomes your new normal," author Robin Sharma eloquently points out. That's sage wisdom in many respects, and it comes down to the New Normal necessitating an expansion of your horizons. The only way to avoid being forever stuck in the muck is to find new hands, as well as old, to help pull you out at the same time you find new souls worthy of your loyalty.

- **Acknowledge small victories.** There's no such thing as a small victory, especially in the face of the crushing defeat so many of us have experienced since the New Normal set in. And celebrating those victories, no matter how insignificant they may seem, makes for a strong counterweight to the defeats we have suffered recently. After all, writes author Paulo Coelho, "The great victory, which appears so simple today, was the result of a series of small victories that went unnoticed."

- **Look beyond the numbers.** Loyalty is not always measurable or quantifiable. It's best suited for the long game, not the short. Placing value in others makes it far more likely they will place value in you. And being loyal to them similarly raises the chances of them being loyal to you when you need them the most. There's nothing wrong with reaching for the brass ring. But sometimes just riding the merry-go-round is its own reward.

FORETHOUGHT

After the life of a Frogman, Steve pictured still walking in mud, but now it's his garden in upstate New York after relocating from Southern California

CHAPTER 11

Yesterday, Today, and Tomorrow

He who exercises no forethought but makes light of his
opponents is sure to be captured by them.

—SUN TZU

In this case, we all share a common opponent that has sought to
capture us in its clutches and has succeeded to a scary degree.
No one can be blamed for a lack of forethought going back to the
early days of the pandemic because we simply lacked the necessary
information to reach an informed conclusion. And even if we'd
had it, our psyches would have fought against willingly upending
our lives; indeed, we only acted to a great extent because restrictions were forced upon us.

That, though, is no longer the case. COVID-19 has receded, but
not the residue it has left behind. And dealing with that residue
will require the kind of forethought we didn't employ at the outset
of the outbreak.

In the SEALs, forethought is rooted in anticipation. "In life, as
in chess," Charles Buxton once wrote, "forethought wins."

And if we've learned anything these past few years, it's that playing checkers is no way to get out of the mud; planning several moves ahead, relying on forethought, is a recipe not only to survive the New Normal but emerge stronger. Even thrive. Play chess instead.

Forethought is defined as a careful consideration of what will be necessary or may happen in the future. Everything I did professionally in my life required forethought. Where was I going next? What was my next phase or position I wanted to be in? Positioning yourself for that next promotion either in rank or job, sometimes one leading to the other—that's forethought. Finding those people who will help you along the way is deeply important. Going it alone isn't usually possible, especially in the military and Special Operations. That's forethought too.

I had a former commanding officer who is now retired from active duty working as a civilian for the Department of Defense, our community's headquarters, just like I was. He was one civilian grade above me but had a very important position. We were now friends, and we surfed together often and always saw each other in the command gym. That doesn't mean I said whatever I pleased to him because we were friends—he still held positional authority over me, and I regarded that closely and respectfully. When we spoke about work, it was usually in the form of mentor and mentee. And in the New Normal, we all find ourselves forced to take on both roles: remaining strong as a mentor to others while we seek out mentors to help figuratively lift us from the mud.

So the mission statement of this chapter is to demonstrate the importance of forethought in responding to the New Normal. Looking toward what's coming instead of just bemoaning what's already been. Yogi Berra once famously said, "The future ain't what it used to be." Well, it's within our power to change that future, though not our past.

What We Never Chose

"Michael," Hyman Roth says to Michael Corleone in *The Godfather, Part II*, "this is the business we have chosen."

In other words, don't complain, don't bemoan your lot in the life you chose. But nobody chose the upheaval and disruption wrought by COVID. Indeed, we are living through what sociologists might call a paradigm shift where we're forced to endure an entirely new model for living our lives. So much has changed, and many of those changes are irrevocable. Life won't be going back to the way it was pre-pandemic tomorrow, the next day, or the day after. In fact, we must face the fact that it may never come back all the way. The best we can do is nurture the wisdom required to accept that and the forethought to deal with it.

In a March 2021 article on the NBC News website entitled "Payment Deferrals Were a Lifeline for Millions During Covid. What Happens When Those End?" Harvard Law School professor Howell Jackson told Adam Edelman that "as the pandemic winds down, there is a lot of debt overhang: deferred rent, deferred mortgages, deferred student loans. We've basically been living in suspended animation until the pandemic ends." Jackson, an expert on financial regulation and consumer protection, went on to say, "And at some point there is going to be an extraordinary number of people out there who are very vulnerable with debt, and we are going to have major debt collection issues.... We have already seen issues during the pandemic with payday lenders."

"These periods of forbearance will eventually end," adds David Silberman, former associate director of the Consumer Financial Protection Bureau. "And when they do, there could be millions of families unable to resume paying mortgages, car payments, credit cards, student loans, who could be at risk of losing their homes, their cars, having their wages and bank accounts garnished, who will struggle to put food on the table and take care of their families."

Wait, there's more.

In the spring of 2021, Daniella Silva writing for NBC News as well postulated that "the pandemic upended the lives of millions of families who suddenly found themselves without a source of income, and experts fear the effects could be long-lasting. Many have gone from enjoying the cultural markers of the middle class—job stability, homeownership, and some disposable income—to teetering on the edge of poverty. According to the US Census Bureau, 115 million people had experienced losses in employment income from the start of the pandemic in March 2020 through spring 2021. And according to a Pew Research Center report released this year, more than 4 in 10 adults say they or someone else in their households had lost jobs or wages since the beginning of the pandemic. Even with unemployment insurance, which struggled with claim delays amid unprecedented demand, and other benefits, the impact could have ramifications for years, economic experts and advocates said."

Just as the overall effects of COVID-19 could last decades.

When the pandemic first broke, I don't know anyone who had the forethought to know how bad it would get or how long it would last. But we need that forethought now more than ever to prepare ourselves for what's coming. The writing's on the wall, as they say; we just need sharp enough vision to read all the letters.

Feed the Soul

When I was in my twenties, I was full of myself, thinking I was better than most because of the things I'd achieved. Being a SEAL and having made it through BUD/S was, in my mind's eye, "the shit." In reality, I was this guy who was insecure about who he was and what he had yet to achieve and uncertain about his future. Would I measure up to those who raised me in my community? What would my legacy be?

On my way out the door for my third deployment with the Teams while we were waiting for our flight at the air terminal in Dover, Delaware, I got pretty liquored up with two other buddies. That same week I interviewed and was approved and selected to attend Green Team that coming summer. Meaning, after I got home from deployment, I was going to DevGru, the very best of the best.

A buddy and platoon mate of mine and I were headed out, catching up with the rest of the platoon who were already overseas. As our flight got delayed (military air is always delayed), we drank more. Well, needless to say, by the time we got onto our flight I was drunk. Not staggering, but nonetheless, I was what I shouldn't have been in the first place: drunk in uniform. There was also an Army Ranger captain on our flight. We were all in uniform, so that's how I know and remember all this. What happened next I am truly ashamed of and embarrassed about. I started giving him shit and announcing to my buddy that there was an "Airborne Ranger from the sky" on our plane. I give major credit to this guy that he didn't just pop me one and put me out for the flight. But he didn't. He was a better man than I. He pulled in close to me and spoke quietly.

"Hey, it's really cool that you're a SEAL. Congratulations. I'm an officer in the military. You're enlisted. Now, shut up and go to sleep. That's an order."

That was pretty much it. When we landed in Naples, Italy, eight hours or so later, I was sober and thankfully had some wits about me, and I apologized to the captain for being such a douchebag. He graciously accepted and we parted ways.

I wasn't much about feeding my soul back then. I worked hard and played hard. I only wanted to be the best operator and the best Teammate I could be. That meant dedication to the trade physically and mentally preparing myself as best I could. What I wasn't doing was building on my depth as an individual and really discovering my intrinsic motivation. The difference between the two is huge.

What I needed to do was ask myself these basic questions: What makes me come alive? What are my strengths? What gives me purpose? Where do I add greatest value? How will I measure my life?

Forethought, in other words. And we all need it today as much as I needed it back then. Chess instead of checkers, remember? Always thinking a few moves ahead.

Matthew Haag wrote this for the *New York Times* in late March of 2021:

> A year after the coronavirus sparked an extraordinary exodus from office buildings, what had seemed like a short-term inconvenience is now clearly becoming a permanent and tectonic shift in how and where people work. Employers and employees have both embraced the advantages of remote work, including lower office costs and greater flexibility for employees, especially those with families. Beyond New York, some of the country's largest cities have yet to see a substantial return of employees, even where there have been less stringent government lockdowns, and some companies have announced that they are not going to have all workers come back all the time. In recent weeks, major corporations, including Ford in Michigan and Target in Minnesota, have said they are giving up significant office space because of their changing workplace practices, while Salesforce, whose headquarters occupies the tallest building in San Francisco, said only a small fraction of its employees will be in the office full time.

That's all part and parcel of a paradigm shift. But we have to shelve the excuses and victimhood and ask ourselves: Where will that shift take me next? And how can I deal with and prepare for that?

I hadn't intended to include the United States Navy SEAL creed in these pages, but its appropriateness in answering those questions and addressing the challenges before us today necessitated a change of heart. Here it is:

- In times of war or uncertainty there is a special breed of warrior ready to answer our Nation's call. Common citizens with uncommon desire to succeed. Forged by adversity, they stand alongside America's finest special operations forces to serve their country, the American people, and protect their way of life. I am that warrior.

- My Trident is a symbol of honor and heritage. Bestowed upon me by the heroes that have gone before, it embodies the trust of those I have sworn to protect. By wearing the Trident I accept the responsibility of my chosen profession and way of life. It is a privilege that I must earn every day.

- My loyalty to Country and Team is beyond reproach. I humbly serve as a guardian to my fellow Americans always ready to defend those who are unable to defend themselves. I do not advertise the nature of my work, nor seek recognition for my actions. I voluntarily accept the inherent hazards of my profession, placing the welfare and security of others before my own.

- I serve with honor on and off the battlefield. The ability to control my emotions and my actions, regardless of circumstance, sets me apart from others. Uncompromising integrity is my standard. My character and honor are steadfast. My word is my bond.

- We expect to lead and be led. In the absence of orders I will take charge, lead my teammates, and accomplish the mission. I lead by example in all situations.

- I will never quit. I persevere and thrive on adversity. My Nation expects me to be physically harder and mentally stronger than my enemies. If knocked down, I will get back up, every time. I will draw on every remaining ounce of strength to protect my teammates and to accomplish our mission. I am never out of the fight.

- We demand discipline. We expect innovation. The lives of my teammates and the success of our mission depend on me--my technical skill, tactical proficiency, and attention to detail. My training is never complete.

- We train for war and fight to win. I stand ready to bring the full spectrum of combat power to bear in order to achieve my mission and the goals established by my country. The execution of my duties will be swift and violent when required yet guided by the very principles that I serve to defend.

- Brave SEALs have fought and died building the proud tradition and feared reputation that I am bound to uphold. In the worst of conditions, the legacy of my teammates steadies my resolve and silently guides my every deed. I will not fail.

- None of us can fail. We've already had too much taken from us with a promise of more to come.

What This Means for You

So much about being a SEAL is being part of a great team, with no shortage of colleagues, friends, and even mentors to choose from. And I believe the whole notion of cultivating your own "teammates" in the same respect is what's called for more than ever in the New Normal.

For instance, being a great friend (I think) makes it easier to find great friends yourself, no matter your age or stage of life. Take it as seriously as the role requires, respect boundaries, and embrace the friendship. In fact, it's easy to make the argument that someone who's mentored others is best positioned for seeking their own mentor as well because they enjoy a deeper understanding of the obligations and responsibilities—a different kind of forethought, in other words.

In a more general sense, you should also have the forethought to know what your monolith in life is. Your capstone. That cherished part of you most likely to be waiting when you reach the other side of the mud. It could be a personal goal, a career goal, maybe even a system of beliefs. It could be faith-, community-, or family-based. Whatever it might be, in looking back, all you need is a mirror. In looking ahead, you need forethought instead.

A Prescription for Healing

- **Find a mentor.** If you don't have a mentor, find one. Seek out the person who can help you, listen to you, and dole out some sage advice or thoughts on whatever you're facing. And if you are a mentor, apply the reverse to your charge.

- **Rekindle those special friendships.** I'm talking about the select few who leave you genuinely appreciative for them being in your life. They make you feel better about yourself and, in a perfect world, the reverse is true as well.

- **Start working on a project you've been putting off.** And don't resist asking for help along the way, should you need it. One of the true unspoken talents these times have brought to life is the willingness and ability to ask for help, a question posed in full recognition that you'd be glad to be the one answering it had the situations been reversed.

- **Help someone.** Seek out a neighbor, friend, or coworker who needs help with something—ideally, someone who's struggling and could really use the hand you're extending. Remember, there are a lot of people out there who have even more trouble accepting help than asking for it. As the proverb says, "Pride goeth before the fall." Truer words have never been spoken.

COMMON SENSE

Steve and his wife Burbara, present day

CHAPTER 12

Tasks, Conditions, and Standards

Common sense is something that everyone needs,
few have, and none think they lack.

—BENJAMIN FRANKLIN

Common sense is a hard term to define exactly, one of those things that you know when you see it. I saw it as a SEAL in the mutual dependency of Teammates in training as well as combat. You're only as good as the person to your right and the person to your left. In my mind, that's the epitome of common sense.

In the game of baseball, it takes a special skill to understand not just who's at bat or how many outs there are. Life, just like in baseball, has so much more to the game than that. As a mentor and Chief in my assault team once told me, "Don't get caught playing checkers while the other guy is playing chess." What he meant was the job is way more complicated than it seems, a fast, dynamic process with lots of moving parts. If you get caught playing checkers while everyone else is playing chess, you'll end up losing every time. Thanks, Mike.

In life nobody sets out to lose, or to get caught playing checkers in a chess match. Most if not all people plan on winning and finishing with a happy, fulfilling life. But what does that mean exactly? Here in America, a lot of people might think that would be finishing with a lot of money to your name while others think it's more about happiness and fulfillment of a satisfying life well lived. I'm of the latter camp. When my wife and I retired, we made sure we could sustain a standard we would enjoy and be okay with. It's not a lavish lifestyle, but we're happy and satisfied. Neither of us came from a lavish lifestyle as children and most certainly didn't live that way as enlisted military or civil servants working for the government.

Task, Conditions, and Standards, or just TCS, are a basic, common sense formula used for training to tasks in a very specific way with a standard to be met. You should learn the specific conditions and standards before training to a task so you understand what the expectation is. That's an established principle of Special Operations, and the mission statement of this chapter is to show how to apply it to everyday life and the New Normal.

TCS

First, let's define our terms.

Task: A clearly defined and measurable activity accomplished by individuals and organizations. Tasks are specific activities that contribute to the accomplishment of requirements.

Conditions: The circumstances and environment in which the task is to be performed, whether it be an environment such as diving or parachuting or a battle skill like shooting and maneuvering.

Standard: The minimum acceptable proficiency required in the performance of the training task under a specific set of conditions. Not just surviving, but accomplishing the task well, proficiently.

174

Those are basic principles, drawn from common sense. Not complicated at all. Indeed, as Lao Tzu once wrote, "Simplicity is the ultimate sophistication." Ask any SEAL if he was right.

So, let's say for example your task, along with three friends, is to change a flat tire on your vehicle. I had to do this once with three other guys from our crew in our assault team. It was hilarious.

The Task: Change the flat tire with the spare as fast and safely as we could using only what we had in our vehicle.

- Loosen the lug nuts.
- Lift the vehicle off the ground.
- Remove the lug nuts and the tire.
- Place the spare tire on the car.
- Replace the lug nuts.
- Lower the car and tighten the lug nuts.
- Get back in the car, turn on the music, and roll back down the road.

The Conditions: Start from inside the car, all seat belts worn and doors and trunk closed. Task is not completed until all persons are back in their original position in the car ready to drive. Remember, safety first!

The Standard: Having never timed ourselves at this before, we gave each person a specific job for the task. The other members of our crew graded and timed our performance while also heckling us to no end. I think it was about four minutes "from soup to nuts," as they say.

Not too bad for having never practiced it. But we were used to doing things in a hastily devised plan and using our skills as an operational unit. We were able to say who was to get the spare tire, who would handle the jack, who was responsible for the lug nuts, etc. We were given one minute while still in the car to come up with a plan. When the "Go!" came, it was game on.

A unit must be tested regularly in order to conduct a self-check on performance, relying again on common sense. Change a flat tire, or take down and clear a target of all opposition, or make a product in an emergent manner for a customer who needs it as soon as possible. The conditions are what your circumstances are at that time, what realistic stressors are to be added to challenge the unit or team.

It's one thing, for example, to run through a target and just shoot 'em up. This is what amateurs do. It's another to clear the target methodically, surgically, and shoot only what you've been directed to, as in, "Shoot only the targets with green triangles that are upside down while in low-light conditions and wearing a gas mask in full kit, employing all TTPs."

Meaning, engage very specific targets by mentally separating the right-side-up green triangles, the blue triangles, the red triangles, and so on while wearing your full combat gear in addition to a gas mask in a dimly lit, thirty-plus-room multistory structure that will demand all of your standard tactics, techniques, and procedures.

The standard is to engage the targets your team was told to engage, under the specific conditions given, and within a designated "time on target"—no lollygagging, people! By training and working to specific standards, it isn't difficult to do just about anything in a very direct and deliberate manner, even while walking in mud. Tests like this heighten the individual and team situational and spatial awareness, not to mention the skills required to execute the most difficult missions required by Special Operations. And the process represents a commonsense dictum that can be applied to areas far beyond the battlefield. Practice, as the saying goes, really does makes perfect.

What set apart the command I spent so much time at from others was the drive they had and the breakneck pace at which they trained and operated. It still holds true today. When we were on Alert Cycle when I first got there in 1987, we trained on Christ-mas Eve day on the shooting range and in the shoot house doing CQC. No slack. We had a three-day weekend and then were back in on Monday "paying our rent." Bad guys don't take days off, so neither could we.

Let's look at a more explicit example of applying the TCS prin-ciples to a specific role within Special Operations to demonstrate how TCS levels of common sense can be applied to everyday tasks as well, some of which have grown significantly more challenging in the New Normal.

I was part of our lead climber cell within my assault team for five years. There were about eight or ten of us total. We would venture out to various rock-climbing locations throughout the United States and climb these incredible natural geologic mas-terpieces during our Specialized Training Cycle, which followed our at-home Alert Cycle. We would sometimes go directly to an offshore gas or oil rig after climbing rock and apply our skill at free-climbing a rig from the water, setting our protective gear (our "pro"—the cams and nuts to clip your rope into in order to prevent you from falling to your death) and getting the rest of the team up and onto the rig for a tactical assault.

My very first trip as a lead climber we were climbing in the Black Hills, Custer State Park, and the Needles in South Dakota and at Devils Tower in Wyoming. I had only been rock climb-ing once before, and that was in France while on a platoon deployment to the Mediterranean. That day's climbing was very gentle and easy, and we learned the basics from a unit of the French Mountain Rescue. Our platoon commander had set it up through our French commando counterparts while we were in the port of Toulon.

The Task: The climbing we were conducting at the Needles and Devils Tower was far more technical and extremely challeng-ing. My personal task was to learn how to ascend vertical rock faces, first by following a teammate, then by leading, and everything that goes into this technical skill set: placing protection, rope management, chasing your route, belaying, and assisting your climbing partner.

The Conditions: Obviously, to get up the damn rock face, utilizing our freshly taught skill set.

The Standard: To complete the task of ascending a rock face successfully by the end of the three-week trip.

This all entailed eighteen days of climbing for eight to nine hours per day with one day of rest per week to allow recovery and to try to get the feeling back in our fingertips.

We were taught by some of the best in North America. Our lead instructor was a guy named Jay, and he assembled a team of three more experts who would coach us in the skill of rock climbing. They demonstrated, then we would do it while they coached. Not all of us were new to climbing. Others on the team, the guys who had been there longer, had already gone through this and were far more capable and skilled than us "new guys." They were cut from the herd and dispatched to go climb what they wanted with a climbing partner and all of their gear. The rest of us stayed with Jay, who was an expert's expert. He was very articulate and systematic. He had managed just about every hard climb in North America, which included alpine mountaineering at Mount Rainier, Denali, Grand Teton, Half Dome, and El Capitan, just to name a few. He'd also climbed Mount Everest and K2, as well as completed many climbs in Patagonia. Needless to say, his résumé was deep.

His fellow guides were just as experienced in the art of rock climbing and mountaineering. One guy, Bob, was also a stuntman who had done some pretty impressive gigs in Hollywood. All of them were impressive in their skill and very capable instructors.

Bob told me he liked teaching SEALs because he usually only had to teach us once, coach us twice, and then sit back and watch. They would usually free-climb alongside us on the easier climbs and talk us through the basics or a sticky situation we may have gotten ourselves in. The physicality of rock climbing wasn't a challenge to us since we were already in top physical condition, and we prepared for the coming trip with specific exercises and workouts. And we learned fast. It wasn't all just ascending the rock face; it was also every other aspect of going up and down a steep mountain and vertical rock face safely with skill.

It's important here to note that the American system of climbing grades is based off the Yosemite Decimal System (YDS), which ranges from class one (hiking) to class five (technical rock climbing). The idea of climbing grades is fairly straightforward, but when applied to bouldering, sport climbing, alpine climbing, ice climbing, or mountaineering, the grades change based on the local climbing area or by the international standard.

By the time we were done with my first trip, my climbing partner, Dave, and I had successfully led and followed each other through various climbs starting with some moderate 5.7s and finished off with El Matador on Devils Tower, a 5.11a five-pitch climb. Not too shabby for two guys who'd never really climbed before. The physical strength and stamina required for a climb like that, let alone at the end of a three-week trip like ours, was incredible. I seriously thought I was in great shape prior to this trip, but by the time we were headed home I was seriously smoked and my ego was in check. I had been humbled.

I came close to dying on that trip as well. Sure, I had taken some falls while both leading and following, but I was tied in, Dave always had me, and we had learned to "stitch up the cracks" like it was second nature. But one particular climb, Soler, a 5.9 two-pitch climb, was the closest I had come to death at this point in my life. We seriously struggled on this climb and traded off multiple times leading and following and falling, testing everything we had learned up until that point. Our coach, Robert, was watching from below and chowing on our food we'd left there. When Dave and I got to the top of the Tower we celebrated with a handshake and entered our names in the logbook that was there to record everyone's successful summit.

We took in the view and started our decent the same way we came up, but this time it was a rappel back down the two pitches we had just climbed. Devils Tower is a rock column, and there isn't a trail to walk down on the back side like some places.

We would have to stop midway down, clip into a wall anchor, and reset our ropes for the second half of the descent. I went first and my job was to rappel down 155 feet or so, locate the wall anchor, and set another piece of pro in order to support myself and Dave and then clip in and belay Dave. One major thing I failed to do was to tie a knot in the last six feet or so of my rope to ensure I didn't let the whole thing go through my hand and plummet the remaining 165 feet to my death.

As I was nearing where I thought the anchor should be so I could clip in, I noticed a very odd feeling in my break hand, like the rope was really light. When I came to a full stop on the rock face to check and see what the deal was, I realized two things: I'd run out of rope, and I'd failed to tie the knot at the end!

I was down to my last few feet of rope and, as I started to look for the anchor I needed to clip in to, I saw that it was about six feet above me. Oh shit! As Dave yelled down asking if I had found the anchor, I was busy using every bit of strength I had left to pull the rope through my rappelling device inch by inch to get within arm's reach of that beautiful anchor I so desperately needed. I stopped what I was doing, locked off what little rope I had, and yelled back up that I had located it and just needed to set the appropriate protection.

What I was really doing was freaking out in my head, forgetting my basic rock climbing TTPs, and scrambling to save my own stupid life by pulling my way to safety. It maybe took only about five minutes, but it seemed like an eternity, and I finally was able to clip into the wall anchor and set the other pro so Dave could rappel down to my location and we could finish our descent. I didn't tell Dave what had happened until we were completely down and had collected all of our ropes and other gear.

Dave gave me an "Oh shit!" as I filled him in on what had happened and then we nervously laughed as we headed back, agreeing to keep it just between us. A guide with one of the other assault team lead climbers had died a year or two prior in a similar incident at Red Rocks near Las Vegas. The kind of man whose death garnered no headlines while the purpose of his life was to keep men like me off the obituary pages.

Our TCS had been completed until the next trip when Freddy, our assault team lead climber, would set up a final climb for us where we made a single-pitch climb led by him, but we were wearing our first-line assault gear and it was at night. That set the bar for us, the assault team, and the command.

I would eventually become our team's Climbing Department head, relieving Freddy as he moved on to the command's training cadre. To push the metaphor a bit, I had started the process on the ground floor and climbed the stairs to the figurative top in this same respect.

TCS for Life

Learning to train and then operate under Tasks, Conditions, and Standards gave us a new perspective on how to manage our own lives. If something didn't work, you made adjustments or discarded that way of doing things. You managed your risk, your swim buddy's risk, and your team's risk all for a greater good, success on the battlefield, or in this case in the battlefield of life.

Running headlong into a situation with blinders on using only your impulsive emotions is no way to go through life or the New Normal. Relationships sometimes go this way, as I learned throughout my life. That's probably why I failed, more than once, but isn't that what life is about? Live, learn, regroup, and then live again, hopefully not to repeat and also only impacting you. But at some point that has to evolve into more educated, less impulsive decision-making. In other words, you have to exercise common sense.

When I bought my first house, I was twenty-four and didn't have a clue as to what I was doing. It's not like buying a car, that's for sure. I didn't negotiate and I didn't seek advice from my older and wiser Teammates who had gone through this already. I paid full asking price and closing costs and ignored what the final cost of home ownership would run me. I almost maxed out my monthly paycheck and drained my savings. My then girlfriend moved in with me and helped with the mortgage, and for a short time we had roommates. My father helped as well and for that I will always be forever grateful.

This was a bad, uneducated, impulsive decision that put me into a financial bind that would last for years. I married my girlfriend, we had two great kids, but we remained in debt. I grew increasingly frustrated and anxious at my circumstance but also knew I had only myself to blame.

Arguably, the one thing I can say I did do right was that I took responsibility for those decisions I made. It may not have been right away, but I did take ownership of those bad decisions that put me and my family in a situation that wasn't ideal. I didn't lead my family unit as I should have. My failure ended in divorce. I learned. I regrouped and moved on, with the awareness that I had failed to apply the commonsense principles of TCS to everyday life.

Getting yourself out of these situations requires teamwork. Not placing blame or pointing fingers. It requires management and adult things like taking control of your finances by eliminating emotional and impulsive spending. If the teamwork fails, or one of the two of you doesn't help to hold up your end of the bargain, the effort and end result of your goal will fail. Grasping the brass ring will no longer be achievable.

I look at this current place we're in with recovery from the pandemic, civil unrest, and unemployment due to the uncontrollable circumstances that were largely out of our control. Are we a country that has failed at our commitment to each other? Can we regroup? I think so.

What This Means for You

We climb a figurative mountain every day of our lives. Sometimes it's an easy walk; other times it's an arduous trek. That's always been the case, but it's taken on added meaning in the New Normal in which the handholds become fewer, the grade steeper, and the face more slippery. Applying the same Tasks, Conditions, and Standards we did to literally climb up a sheer rock face can be an effective strategy in climbing out of the figurative muck.

Taking control of our personal lives, stopping our blame game, and understanding that everyone is going through this together are commonsense principles we need to apply now more than ever. Essentially, it comes down to being a decent human and countryman to each other. Being a good citizen doesn't just mean not breaking the law. It involves these other actions that help to uplift your community and make it better than how you came into it. Because the greater good is what's best for the individual good. Another commonsense principle.

Life isn't always easy, and nobody ever promised it would be. Reliving the past does nobody any good. All it does is reopen old wounds that should have been left alone to heal.

Cultivating a mindset that will allow you to make peace with your past mistakes and bring quiet and happiness into where you are now doesn't seem like a natural or sometimes easy path to recovery from a really shitty stretch of time, but it can be, I promise. Especially now when things seem so overwhelming.

Our rock-climbing training, in that respect, becomes an apt metaphor for the New Normal, as there are times when we all face the sense that we're free-climbing without a partner or rope to support us. So much of life is about looking up at what's ahead of you without peering down at the vast abyss awaiting if you slip. Along with everything else, COVID-19 has left us fearing that abyss and feeling our grip on life grow more and more precarious. So, I thought it would be a good idea in this final chapter to assemble some commonsense principles you can apply to pretty much anything, but especially everyday life.

Push out the negative thoughts or reject them as they come along and step forward with courage, no matter your circumstance.

Stop trying to get even with your perceived enemies and try taking that road less traveled, the high road. Going after anyone with revenge is useless. It accomplishes nothing.

Renting your successes and paying that rent, which comes due every day, is one of the best approaches to getting out of the slog. And never stop building on your success, whether it be raising and cultivating a great family or business or just being the most kick-ass employee anyone has ever seen in that company or organization. You don't have to be the boss to be successful. You just have to be the boss of yourself, and that's where commonsense TCS comes in.

If you fail, own it, learn from it, don't repeat it, and move on. All of this may seem really simplistic, but I've applied these very same principles to my life and have prospered not in just mental well-being but in overall health, as well as personal victories and accomplishments.

A Prescription for Healing

But common sense doesn't stop there in this regard. There are also additional principles you can apply that summon the same Tasks, Conditions, and Standards thinking.

- **Manage information.** "Everybody gets so much information all day long," Gertrude Stein once wrote, "that they lose their common sense." Information overload forces us to overthink as opposed to relying on common sense. And Stein uttered that quote nearly a century ago, long before the age of social media and email. But so much of the information we consume that way can be discouraging and negative. This is not a time to be further discouraged, and we certainly don't need any more negativity in our lives. So, manage your consumption of information and be careful of its content.

- **Make common sense your superpower.** I saw a T-shirt once that read, "Common sense is so rare these days, it should be classified as a superpower." Indeed, we're walking in mud now because our leaders failed to apply commonsense TCS principles during the early months of COVID, but that doesn't mean you should follow their lead. Applying logic and reason to any challenge, pushing aside the emotion and overreaction, is a great tactic to emerge from the mud.

- **Have a plan.** Yes, you have to be flexible, willing to change on the fly. But you can't alter a plan if you don't have one to start with. That might be a plan to get you back to where you were pre-COVID. Or it might be a plan to adjust to the framework of the New Normal that's been imposed upon you.

- **Work with a team.** These times cry out for the polar opposite of going it alone. Let's say you have a skill set to start a business but not the funding. So, you need to bring someone into your circle who brings that, either a resource or skill you don't have, to the table. Knowing what you need is great, but knowing where to find it and from whom is even greater.

- **Be resilient.** Resilience in the case of the New Normal means looking forward to what's ahead and not looking back to where you were before. Kind of like Lot's wife in the Bible who becomes a pillar of salt after she looks back at Sodom. A perfect parable for the need to be resilient while facing the future.

- **Reach the mountaintop.** "The man on the top of the mountain didn't fall there," Vince Lombardi once said. And getting to the top, or back to the top, was no accident either. It took planning, foresight, and adhering to the principles of TCS to get there. But here's the thing. Climbing that one mountain merely positions you to climb the next. So, celebrate the task's completion but then be ready to conquer the next one. Resting on your laurels means sinking deeper into the mud.

Frogman Rules

Live a good life. If there are gods and they are just, then they
will not care how devout you have been but will welcome you
based on the virtues you have lived by. If there are gods, but
unjust, then you should not want to worship them. If there are
no gods, then you will be gone but will have lived a noble life
that will live on in the memories of your loved ones.

—MARCUS AURELIUS

You could categorize this quote in the "shut up and be a good
person" section of life advice. I'm a fan of it. I hope you are too.

Don't you hate those books that finish with a recap of all the
themes covered as if you weren't paying attention the first time?
Don't worry, I'm not going to do that here. Instead, I'm going to
offer a general breakdown of the Ten Essential Qualities of an
Underwater Demolition Man. These aren't just qualities, though;
they're principles to live by in times both good and bad, whether
you're sitting on the beach or walking in the mud. But they apply
in especially pointed, relevant fashion to the latter.

Most pointedly for our case, and what makes this a fitting way
to end our journey together, is that applying the Ten Qualities to

everyday life gets you to the other side. The mud won't seem so thick, the slog not so slow, the fatigue not so great. You'll find your-self looking up and ahead instead of down at your shoes wedged in the muck weighing you down. In stark contrast to that, the Ten Qualities can uplift you and serve as a guide to not just get to the other side but to avoid having to walk in mud ever again.

1. PRIDE: In yourself, in your team, in the amphibious force, and in the Navy, and most important, pride in developing the same pride in subordinates.

> **Ownership.** People want to take pride in things that are close to them. They also take pride in their own personal achieve-ments. Give the members of your family, organization, or team something to take ownership in, whether it's setting up the cleaning duties around the house, collateral job assignments that have to be done, a project, or the weekly meeting agenda. This has two benefits. First, they will surprise you with what they can accomplish. Second, the devil finds work in idle hands. High-performance individuals need to focus their energy.

> **Humility.** Never be too big or important to do the small things that need to be done. Humble people work to better them-selves even when things are going well. Setting your ego aside allows you to be open to other people's ideas or methods that may be better than your own. And let's face it, COVID and its aftershocks have humbled all of us to some degree, making us feel small and ineffective in its face. We don't need to feel big; we just need to feel as big as we did before the world closed right before our eyes.

> During my first Specialized Training Cycle in the assault team, I was sent to EMT school—not exactly the tier-one oper-ator training I expected. The other guys were going climbing, shooting, tactical driving, and the like. I was ass-hurt but more

importantly, the purpose was never explained to me. A team-mate and friend pulled me aside at one point and explained to me the purpose, as well as reminded me to be professional about it all. As it would turn out, two months later I was using those newly acquired EMT skills to render aid to a fellow operator who got seriously injured by a grenade in a training accident. He lost the sight in his eye, but it could have been far worse. That was the purpose. That EMT training would con-tinue to be a benefit throughout my career.

2. LOYALTY: Up and down, in action and word.

Aligned values. Whether you have a big team, a large company, or just your family, if the values aren't aligned it's going to be a disaster. Getting everyone on board can be hard, especially if you're the new leader. Occasionally it's good to review what those values are, tweak them if you need to, and then present them to the team as the leader. Make them simple and easy to repeat back if needed.

In the family unit this needs to be done constantly, espe-cially when the kids are young, but in ways that they don't perceive as a lecture. My father wasn't good at this and neither was I. Everything seemed to be a lecture. But I later saw value in his words, so maybe if they were presented in a different way or context, it might have worked. Make it conversational and not one-sided. Give people a voice and yours will reso-nate louder.

Honor. As defined by demonstrating integrity and loyalty and putting the needs of the team or your family higher than your own. In the team or operational concept, you must have a posi-tive reputation and actively further the reputation of the team. Refining your personal respectability will give you a lot of credit, earning respect from those above and below you on the team or in the chain of command. This applies to everything you do in daily life, not just Special Operations.

3. SINCERITY: In all you do.

Perseverance. This is also where grit is applied. You're resisting short-term temptations for long-term gain. That willingness to put it on the line for success of the mission and leaving an empty gas tank on the battlefield. Whether it be with your unit and brothers in arms, your family unit, the company, or a sports team, having sincerity in what you're doing is critical for success. The phrase "my word is my bond" gets thrown around a lot, enough to seem clichéd at times. It's nonetheless a crucial attribute to not just getting out of the mud but positioning yourself to help others work their way out as well. Nothing wrong with being that helping hand that lifts them the final bit of the way.

Sincerity conveys passion and perseverance for long-term and meaningful goals. It's also defined as the ability to persist in something you feel passionate about and persevere when you face obstacles. This kind of passion is not about intense emotions or infatuation. When deciding to enter into a profession or any endeavor, you have to accept that it's for the long haul and that obstacles will come along. It's grit that'll get you through those tough times. That's true for all personal life choices. It's not always roses, unicorns, and rainbows.

Intrinsic motivation. This means having a clear life purpose that aligns with your personal passions, values, and goals. As a leader, you cannot expect everyone to be as passionate about what you're doing as you are. It's rare that you find that and as teams get bigger, you start to lose the passion among some of your people. That's when you rely on your "core believers" to keep the spirit and passion alive. Your "lieutenants" help reinforce the message and drive that train. So not only do you need to find the right mentors to follow but you also need to be discerning in selecting those who follow you the closest. Whose company do you enjoy the most? Who can you trust the most? Who do you find the most sincere? These are the people you should surround yourself with in the New Normal.

It's not always a perfect fit. If your values don't align with your organization, that doesn't make you a bad person. Maybe the right questions weren't asked during the recruiting process, or maybe the organization just wants to move in another direction.

Some people want to join a team or company because they think it's the cool thing to do, especially in high school sports or the military. Sometimes enthusiasm is mistaken for capability. First, though, you must give them the chance to reflect and ask themselves if they're the right fit and if they really want to be there. If the answer is no, then it's simple and they will self-deselect, hopefully. If not, and they place the blame on you for the lack of their performance, then it's time to tell them, "Put your finger in a cup of water, pull it out, and see how long it takes to fill back up. That's how quickly you'll be missed." Tough words, but it works...most times. Often, if the individual believes in the mission, they will accept their new role within the organization or team and hopefully learn from that experience and own what got them reassigned.

4. RESPONSIBILITY: You have it, so act accordingly and live up to it.

Team culture and family culture. At a foundational level, culture is not what you believe, it's how you behave. What are the behaviors and traits that are going to lead to whatever outcome you want for your team or your family? Does everyone "ride for the brand"? Are they true followers and understand the mission, or do some of them work to undermine your efforts? Is there that individual in the office who seems to always be out of sync when it comes to team projects or even the overall mission? Sometimes all it takes is just one person to throw the whole thing sideways.

What prevents or inhibits performance? It's not usually a lack of desire but rather a lack of clarity in the environment and what the realistic expectations are. The mission, in other words. As a leader you need to set those expectations early and remind and repeat often in various ways. Never go for the knockout punch. It's the repeated jabs that make the biggest impact.

I failed at reinforcing my team culture the right way when I was the Assault Team Chief from 1999 to 2001. I took the opportunity to reinforce the narrative of the command vision, the command policies, but as much as I tried, I couldn't pull it off because I wasn't throwing enough jabs. I was relieved, as was my Team Leader, for what I would say was the "pirate culture" of the team; those who did what they pleased when they left the confines of the command, no matter how much I preached and lectured against that behavior. It wasn't my fault, but it was my responsibility. That's a crucial distinction and one you should always keep in mind.

5. LEADERSHIP: You are the leader in title, so be sure you are in deed as well.

Self-rule. I'm not going to follow someone who can't lead their way out of a wet paper bag. To be a leader, it's essential that you own your own shit first. Ownership and accountability for yourself always comes first. My father was a great example of this, which I wish I would have followed when I was younger.

I was led astray by an ideal and my own misguided beliefs. I didn't feed my soul the way I should have and fell short on rent more days than I can remember. I celebrated my successes far longer than I should have and forgot that I needed to earn the respect of those closest to me, my peers, friends, and superiors, every day. If you can't lead yourself, you can't lead others. And the person helping others in their walk through the mud will feel their own slog get easier.

Being the leader. You have to be a leader the people in your life want to follow into the (metaphorical) fight. Make sure they are willing to perform and leave the tank empty every day alongside you, whether they be your teammates, family, or subordinates at work. Those most deserving of a helping hand are those willing to extend theirs too.

6. EXAMPLE: You always set it. Be sure it's good.

Core values. Nobody is above the standard. People are watching the leaders. If you want people to act and behave in the best possible way, you better act that way yourself. There were several times I fell short on this and said or did things that were below the standard that I demanded. We all stumble. Remember to identify what happened, accept and own it, and move on. Fortunately for me, I had people close to me who would be brutally honest and tell me I screwed up. Beating yourself up over it does nobody any good.

Define where you want to go ethically, then figure out the behaviors that are going to help you get there. What you say as a leader is extremely important. Your followers, your team, your family are listening whether you think they are or not. Choose your words wisely. Don't offend, demean, embarrass, or admonish anyone in public. Doing so will create resentment and most times irreparable damage.

Discipline. Discipline is about maintaining and demonstrating self-control in all things in your life. Discipline means setting an example. It means being the first one to arrive and the last one to leave. Discipline is surgical precision in the little things because when the little things are perfect, the big things seem to just fall into place. It means even the most menial tasks are completed with laser focus and attention to detail.

7. FORETHOUGHT: Cultivate the habit and exercise it.

Mission before ego. You are not above any task or objective. Whatever that task entails, you must complete it with extreme attention to detail and perfection. If setting up the range for the team is your objective, complete it with the utmost precision and efficiency. If it means doing a smaller, seemingly less important task in order to complete the overall objective, then do it. The job wouldn't have been given to you if the confidence wasn't there that you could be trusted to do it.

Balance. These traits all require balance; without balance, all of them can turn from positive to negative. Pride can be good and bad, competition can be good and bad, even communication can be good and bad. As leaders and subordinates, you must constantly assess where you and your team are at and adjust accordingly. Your team will be at its best when balanced.

Mission preparation. Going on a mission is the end of an awfully long process. It's all about training, the preparation, and getting to know your team and yourself. The "Big Seven Philosophy," comprised of marksmanship, physical training, medical training, small-unit tactics, mobility, teamwork, and leadership, serve as supporters of the success of the individual operator and ultimately the team.

8. FAIRNESS: Be absolutely fair and square with subordinates; there is no other standard.

Praise. Napoleon Bonaparte said, "A soldier will fight long and hard for a bit of colored ribbon." Praise should be deserved and not handed out arbitrarily, but if it's deserved, your praise will carry more weight. When appropriate, deliver praise in public. Not all praise warrants a group or public gathering, and if the individual doesn't like public adoration, then do it privately and always with sincerity.

Appraisals. Provide honest, constructive feedback on performance in the form of 360-degree evaluations. An honest assessment from those you serve, your peers, and your leadership will help you be a more effective leader and follower. If you're concerned about what your subordinates will say, then you're doing something wrong. Set your ego aside, because leadership is not about you; it's about your service to them, your team. Great leaders create better leaders.

9. SEAMANSHIP: Only a man who is a competent seaman can truly command respect.

Competence. Be skillful at what you do, whether it be at work or at home. Developing those skills takes time, but through training and practice it arrives. Don't hesitate to seek help if something is too hard or you just don't know the answer or the solution to a problem. Those skills you need to be the best at your job or in life are learned; nothing happens overnight or intuitively. Take the time to learn and be competent. Become vested in your unit, company, or tribe. Adapt to their culture and they will embrace you. "It's not the ship so much as the skillful sailing that assures the prosperous voyage," George William Curtis once said.

Strength. This virtue doesn't just refer to raw strength, it refers to all things relating to physical, intellectual, and emotional fitness. Your physical fitness is the foundation to your mindset and should be maintained to maximize self-esteem, leaving you feeling good about yourself and affecting something over which you have control.

Intellectual fitness is the ability to think critically about issues, having an active and curious mind, and using that to expand your own knowledge within your profession.

Emotional fitness refers to your ability to feel and trust the full array of your emotions, to more efficiently create the circumstances, success, and "flow" we desire in life.

Courage. You must have the mental quality that recognizes fear of danger but enables you to proceed in the face of danger with calmness and firmness. "Courage," wrote Ernest Hemingway, "is grace under pressure."

Character. Align your behaviors with personal and organizational core values. Make yourself a role model who drives the norms. More than any other trait, your character defines and determines who you are. And when character is tested, as it has been first by COVID and now the New Normal it has left behind, we learn who a person is at their very core. Be the person who excels when tested, who wants to be the person at the head of the line.

10. COMMON SENSE: There is no substitute, so use it.

Mastery. Understanding, judgment, wisdom, knowledge, and technical proficiency are essential to being a well-rounded operator in the SOF world, but those traits apply to other career fields. In any form of special operations or first responder careers, you have to master technology, strategy, and tactics, just to name a few. The same applies to the civilian world the vast majority find ourselves a part of. Only by understanding and knowing the rules can you master the game.

Self-concept clarity. As a leader, being able to generate an accurate description of yourself through self-reflection is vital. Recognizing your strengths and skill sets, yes, but also your weaknesses. Being able to leverage the things you're really good at as well as the people who follow you, while maintaining a keen, reflective awareness of the areas where you're not as strong as you want to be—that's key.

Understanding your own self and capabilities and presenting that outwardly is sometimes hard. That's why we need to follow first and learn. Often, the great leaders make the best followers.

Where This Leaves Us

Walking in mud is a slow, arduous slog. But here are a few other general principles to keep in mind no matter how far you are from the end or how thick the mud might be.

Speak once and listen twice. Probably the best rule for a leader, teacher, and parent. Always listen for the return question or comment, and be patient. I think this is sometimes lost in the current world we live in, but persistent intrusive leadership and mentorship is crucial. I know I could have applied this more effectively when I was a much younger leader and parent. Where's the time machine when you need it?

Build gravitas. Confidence and self-esteem as a leader comes from living the behaviors that are core to high performance. Taking the job and mission seriously and with focus can be contagious and lead to success.

Exhibit teamwork. What's your ability to mentor others? Everyone's got a superpower. What can you contribute to the greater mission? Ask yourself, "What can I bring today that's going to add value to the team?" Live like the rent is due every day, not just at the end of the month.

Lay the foundation. If you have the foundation right, and everyone understands what the standards are, that is how you unlock all the things that make a magical culture and highly successful team. This doesn't happen overnight. It requires work.

Know your team. Know your family. You *must* have contact with the people you are leading. You need to understand the folks in your organization, and you can't possibly know your people unless you get down into the trenches and talk to them and, more importantly, listen to them. This is called "intrusive leadership." Do it often enough and with random frequency and you will begin to understand what makes your team click. Get invested and energized by being with them.

It also works at home. Don't let the kids walk in the door without engaging them, even if it's only for a minute or two. Ask them to take the earbuds out and see what they're up to. Ask how their day went. Listen. This is how you know what's happening in their life.

Learn visualization. Have a situation coming up that you've been dreading? Sit in a chair, close your eyes, and imagine exactly what you're going to do. You're going to live it in your brain before you actually do it, and then you go through all the "what ifs." This technique is important and can be applied to anything. Think of scenarios that wouldn't normally come to mind, what could happen, and what you can do to mitigate it. Tremendously successful people utilize this technique for every aspect of their life.

Be disciplined. We had a saying in the Teams: "If you're just in time for a meeting, you're late." My Chief always told me to be at least five minutes early and have a notebook and pen to take notes, always. This helps to develop discipline in other things as well. The unkempt individual or desk displays a person who is unorganized and, I'm willing to bet, late for meetings, disorganized in tasks and approaches to projects. This would also beg the question: Do they care about the job, the team, and the mission?

Be assertive. Effectively expressing yourself and standing up for your point of view shows you have confidence and respect for yourself. Being assertive also demonstrates you respect the beliefs and interests of others.

Be decisive. You should be able to make prompt, appropriate decisions in non-stressful environments as well as tense, uncertain, and rapidly evolving dynamic situations. General George S. Patton said, "A good plan, violently executed now, is better than a perfect plan next week." Avoid "paralysis by analysis" and prioritize and execute on decisions. It's easier explained in simple terms as "failure to react in response to overthought." Don't overthink.

Find what works for you. This is done through success and failure. Learn from your failures and turn those failures into successes.

A Final Prescription

Which brings us to the end. This book, in many respects, contains the sum total of what I learned in my twenty-six years as a Navy

SEAL and thirty-seven years in Special Operations. From the day I found those Ten Essential Qualities of an Underwater Demolition Man, I've never stopped learning—not just about what I needed to be part of successful operations, but also about myself. And I've enjoyed weaving so many of my experiences into these pages, especially the challenges and setbacks, in the hope you will see how I emerged from them and learn the lessons my training and service taught me. And if I learned nothing else over all those years, it was this pearl of wisdom from Henry Ford:

> "When everything seems to be going against you, remember that the airplane takes off against the wind, not with it."

Walking in mud is never easy and never fun. If you're brave enough to start, though, you'll be strong enough to get to the other side. So, I close this book with the eager hope that its content will help you in that task. Once the journey is complete, the mud will dry and a good washing will make your shoes look good as new, maybe even better.

Here's hoping the same can be said of you and that your next walk is toward the future that awaits.